When
Should We Confirm?

Font and Table Series

The *Font and Table Series* offers pastoral perspectives on
Christian baptism, confirmation and eucharist. Other titles in the series are:

A Catechumenate Needs Everybody: Study Guides for Parish Ministers

An Easter Sourcebook: The Fifty Days

At That Time: Cycles and Seasons in the Life of a Christian

Baptism Is a Beginning

Before and After Baptism: The Work of Teachers and Catechists

Commentaries on the Rite of Christian Initiation of Adults

Confirmation: A Parish Celebration

Finding and Forming Sponsors and Godparents

Guide for Sponsors

How Does a Person Become a Catholic?

How to Form a Catechumenate Team

Infant Baptism in the Parish: Understanding the Rite

Parish Catechumenate: Pastors, Presiders, Preachers

Welcoming the New Catholic

Related and available through Liturgy Training Publications:

The Rite of Christian Initiation of Adults (Ritual Edition)
The Rite of Christian Initiation of Adults (Study Edition)

When Should We Confirm?

THE ORDER OF INITIATION

Edited by James A. Wilde

Authors

Frank D. Almade

Geoffrey Steel

John R. Roach

William H. Bullock

Richard P. Moudry

Linda Gaupin

Liturgy Training Publications

© 1989, Archdiocese of Chicago. All rights reserved. Liturgy Training Publications, 1800 North Hermitage Avenue, Chicago IL 60622-1101; Editorial: 312/486-8970 Orders: 312/486-7008

Printed in the United States of America
Art: Linda Ekstrom
Design: Ana M. Stephenson
ISBN 0-930467-84-1

My dear children,
by your baptism you have been born again in Christ
and you have become members of Christ and of his priestly people.
Now you are to share
in the outpouring of the Holy Spirit among us,
the Spirit sent by the Lord upon his apostles at Pentecost
and given by them and their successors to the baptized.

The promised strength of the Holy Spirit,
which you are to receive,
will make you more like Christ
and help you to be witnesses
to his suffering, death and resurrection.
It will strengthen you to be active members of the church
and to build up the body of Christ in faith and love.

—The Invitation to Be Confirmed (RCIA, 233, 324, 589)

Contents

INTRODUCTION

Introduction: Breathe the Fresh Air

JAMES A. WILDE

FIRST, a disclaimer. The title of these volumes on the sacrament of confirmation, "When Should We Confirm?" is not the first question to pose. The age of confirmation is determined by the nature of confirmation. Only when that sacrament is understood historically, theologically, liturgically and pastorally does one ask "When?" The reason for the title is that it identifies a big concern on the minds of a lot of people. It addresses what is really one of the last questions.

When Should We Confirm? The Order of Initiation makes one point. From Sacred Scripture, the documents of the Second Vatican Council, liturgical and canon law, history, theology and, most of all, from pastoral practice, this volume shows that the normative order of initiatory sacraments in the church—baptism, confirmation, eucharist—is expected and possible.

A follow-up volume will take on what the present volume puts to one side: the question of adolescents. It will discuss from many of the same perspectives the potential for rites of affirmation, passage, maturity and personal commitment for teenagers and, indeed, for all

Christians. The pastoral needs and possibilities in this area are enormous.

Chapter 1 reflects a diocesan attempt to restore the original order of the sacraments of initiation. Frank D. Almade, a presbyter of the diocese of Pittsburgh, was commissioned in 1986 by the local Ordinary—then Bishop Anthony Bevilacqua—to set up a committee to study, deliberate and make a proposal for diocesan policy. Almade selected ordained and nonordained persons with expertise in liturgy, catechesis, canon law, theology, pastoral care and child development. Their research and proposal is reprinted here.

Chapter 2 is a report, commentary and evaluation of the restoration of the original order of the initiatory sacraments in the diocese of Salford, which comprises the greater metropolitan area of Manchester, England. The study by Geoffrey Steel, presbyter and seminary professor of liturgy at Ushaw College, Durham, England, provides accurate background, feedback from many sources and constructive suggestions for solving some of the pastoral problems that did or that could arise. It was the Ordinary, Patrick Kelly, bishop of Salford, who, with the guidance of the Vatican Congregation for Divine Worship, took the initiative. Salford's nonoptional plan for parishes has just completed its first cycle, and Steel's report sensitively and critically places a very high value on what is taking place.

Chapter 3 is the confirmation section of *Initiation Sacraments: Guidelines for the Archdiocese of Saint Paul and Minneapolis.* Diocesan policy, in place since early 1987, restores the order of baptism, confirmation, eucharist—but also leaves parishes the option to confirm teenagers after first communion according to the practice begun by Pope Pius X in 1910. The guidelines are printed here because they are liturgically enlightened, catechetically sensitive and pastorally balanced—at the same time. Such guidelines are already in place in other dioceses of Canada, Australia, England and the United States. We thank John R. Roach, archbishop of Saint Paul and Minneapolis, William H. Bullock, then auxiliary bishop and chairperson of the committee on sacraments, now, bishop of Des Moines, Iowa, and the whole church of the Twin Cities for their example.

Chapter 4 brings the issues down to a local parish, that of Christ the King in Minneapolis. Pastor Richard Moudry, catechetical director Richelle Pearl-Koller and the staff and church of Christ the King have worked together since 1982 to restore and refine the process of initiation. In his report, Moudry explains why and how the changes took place. Catechesis of the whole parish over a long period of time and a pastoral team that held strong to a vision were the key ingredients that made the difference in the assembly.

Chapter 5 seeks for confirmation what the decree *Quam Singulari* of Pope Pius x accomplished for first communion in 1910. Its author, Linda Gaupin, CDP, directs the office of worship and also works with parishes to implement the RCIA for the diocese of Wilmington. This chapter flows from the doctoral work she completed on sacramental catechesis under Berard L. Marthaler, OFM CONV at the Catholic University of America. She is on the graduate faculty of LaSalle University, Philadelphia, and she has written numerous articles on liturgical and sacramental catechesis in scholarly, pastoral and popular collections and journals.

There is indeed a ground swell about confirmation all around the globe. Inspired by the Holy Spirit through the Second Vatican Council, liturgical renewal, the restored catechumenate and those marvelous persons called children or young people, the church is breathing fresh air. Breathe it in deep.

CHAPTER 1

Age for Confirmation: A Proposal

FRANK D. ALMADE

THIS DOCUMENT is the result of a study committee on the age for confirmation for the diocese of Pittsburgh. The committee, chaired by Frank D. Almade, included Myles Eric Diskin, Yvonne Hennigan, Richard McLane, Theresa Orlando, Patricia Prince, Joanne Shaner, Gerald Snyder and Annetta Wallace. It completed its work October 30, 1986.

After study, consultation and deliberation, the members of the committee concluded that the question of the appropriate age for confirmation is best seen in the context of the sacraments of initiation: baptism–confirmation–eucharist. Its recommendation is for the diocese of Pittsburgh to restore this ancient order in the celebration of these sacraments for children baptized in infancy. Practical conclusions follow concerning liturgy, catechesis and the program for implementing this recommendation within five years.

The committee examined what the official documents of the Catholic church teach about the revision of the sacraments of initiation, especially confirmation. In addition to the documents, members of the

9

committee consulted theologians, canon lawyers, pastors, liturgists, religious educators, parents, children and young people.

Liturgical Considerations

The Second Vatican Council stated that the rite of confirmation should be revised in order to make clearer "the intimate connection of this sacrament with the whole of Christian initiation" (*Constitution on the Sacred Liturgy* [CSL], 71).

In all of the ritual texts that derive from the CSL, confirmation is clearly identified as one of the church's initiation gestures, one of the sacramental signs that bespeak and accomplish incorporation into the community of Christians and the relationship that they have with God. Confirmation is never spoken of as anything other than "becoming a member" of Christ and the church. Confirmation does not celebrate one's entrance into a "special" vocation nor into a role of exceptional devotion or witness. Along with baptism and eucharist, confirmation ritualizes *entrance into* Christian life rather than any particular accomplishments or fulfillment of that life.

The Apostolic Constitution, *Divinae consortium naturae* (DCN, which, because of its brevity, has no paragraph numbers in the American English versions) of Pope Paul VI, August 15, 1971, by which the Congregation for Divine Worship defined the matter and altered the form of confirmation, speaks about the specific importance of confirmation for sacramental initiation through which the faithful "as members of the living Christ are incorporated into him and made like him through baptism and through confirmation and the eucharist" (quoting the Second Vatican Council's "Decree on the Church's Missionary Activity," 36).

The revised Rite of Confirmation (RC; August 15, 1971) of the Congregation for Divine Worship speaks of handing on to the baptized the special gift of the Holy Spirit. Thus the initiation into the Christian life is completed so that believers are strengthened by power from heaven, made true witnesses of Christ in word and deed and bound more closely to the church.

This special gift of the Holy Spirit "completes baptism, therefore, but it is eucharist that rounds out the initiation cycle." As Pope Paul states:

> The faithful are born anew by baptism, strengthened by the
> sacrament of confirmation and finally are sustained by the food of
> eternal life in the eucharist. (DCN)

The same text discusses some of the early rituals of Christian initiation and the place in them of elements later distinctly recognized as the sacrament of confirmation. After the baptismal washing and before the eucharistic meal, the performance of many rites is indicated, such as anointing, the laying on of hands and consignation.

Thus emerged the traditional "order" of the sacraments of initiation. The document that introduces all of the particular rituals of initiation articulates this order twice in its opening paragraphs:

> Through the sacraments of Christian initiation men and women are
> freed from the power of darkness. With Christ they die, are buried,
> and rise again. They receive the Spirit of adoption which makes
> them God's sons and daughters and, with the entire people of God,
> they celebrate the memorial of the Lord's death and resurrection.
>
> Through baptism men and women are incorporated into
> Christ . . . are formed into God's people . . . and are the children
> of God. Signed with the gift of the Spirit in confirmation,
> Christians more perfectly become the image of their
> Lord. . . . They bear witness to him . . . and work for the
> building up of the body of Christ.
>
> Finally, they come to the table of the eucharist to eat the flesh and
> drink the blood of the Son of Man . . . and show forth the unity of
> God's people. Thus the three sacraments of Christian initiation
> closely combine to bring the faithful to the full stature of Christ.
> (*Christian Initiation: General Introduction* [CI:GI], 1–2)

"Full stature" may here be best understood in the sense of full status as a "Christian person." It is not dependent on one's chronological or intellectual maturity any more than one's status as a human person is dependent upon these things. The Thomistic understanding of the "maturity of faith" conferred by confirmation applies even to confirmed *infants.*

PURPOSE OR EFFECT OF CONFIRMATION

The whole process of Christian initiation enables an individual to have the status of a Christian person, with all its inherent dignity and responsibility. The historical separation of the sacramental gestures of washing, sealing and sharing the meal has led us to the place where we are accustomed to assigning separate purposes and effects to each of the three major gestures. Some such assignments may be difficult to sustain theologically, yet there is a liturgical foundation here. Sacraments are, by nature, signs, and signs "operate" by evocation. It is therefore understandable how one or another ritual gesture may evoke a particular set of images or recognitions among the celebrants.

In the case of Christian initiation those recognitions reveal various dimensions of a single reality: being in Christ. To speak about the "meaning" and "effect" of confirmation is actually to speak about the whole reality of Christian initiation—as it is seen through the words and gestures of that particular sacramental action. To ask "When should we confirm?" is, in fact, simply part of the larger question "When should we initiate?" The "purpose" of confirmation is limited by that larger purpose.

THE PRIMARY EFFECT IS ECCLESIAL

Sacramental "recognitions" happen first of all in the community as a whole and then in the newly baptized—much as the identity and promise of a new child in the family is felt first in the family, as such, then "celebrated" and shared with the new member. This refers to what is known as the "ecclesial effect" of a sacrament, the one out of which arises any effect on particular individuals. Though the presence, for example, of one to be initiated, ordained or reconciled is the occasion for the church's celebration, through that action something happens to the *church:* Its faith is embodied in such a way as to allow a new outpouring of divine grace within the community and for that chosen one.

When this ecclesial effect is overlooked, then sacraments can be mistaken as technical operations upon individuals. We will ask "What does this 'do' to the individual?" before we have asked "What does this 'mean' to the church?" In the sacraments of initiation this ecclesial meaning is all the more critical because these sacraments celebrate precisely what this or these individuals mean to the church of God.

NOTHING MORE AND NOTHING LESS THAN THE *BEGINNING*

There can be various answers to the question of how and over what period incorporation into the church takes place for adults or for children. It should be clear, however, that what is taking place is, in fact, *original formation,* the process by which one can be recognized as fully "one of us" in Christ.

THE END OF THE BEGINNING: EUCHARIST

In the ensemble of the church's initiation gestures, the one that most clearly acknowledges the "now-you-are-one-with-us" dimension is the welcome to the table, the sharing of the eucharist. In it the body of Christ (sacrament) is the food for the body of Christ (church). Because of what this sign means to the *church,* it comes to mean something for those who are invited to have a part in it, even the youngest or most handicapped members. This "eucharistic completion" of baptism is expressed by Pope Paul VI when, after speaking of the baptismal dignity and the confirmation endowment, he says:

> Finally, confirmation is so closely linked with the holy eucharist
> that the faithful, after being signed by holy baptism and
> confirmation, are *incorporated fully* into the body of Christ by
> participation in the eucharist. (DCN)

The RC encourages celebration of confirmation within the Mass, not to multiply Masses but because Christian initiation "reaches its culmination in the communion of the body and blood of Christ" (DCN). The same norm is quite explicit: "The newly confirmed should therefore participate in the eucharist *which completes their Christian initiation*" (RC, 13). This paragraph in the ritual also envisions the possibility that the confirmands may be children who will receive their first communion at yet a later time. In such a case, the eucharist is *not* celebrated (cf. RC, 13). Though it is never denied, there is, in fact, no suggestion in the RC that the unconfirmed would have had previous access to the eucharist.

THE MINISTRY OF THE BISHOP

The liturgical history of initiation reveals how different ministries within the community were involved in the celebration of the rites. There is early evidence of a central position that the bishop held in receiving and affirming the newly baptized in the midst of the gathered community. His role can be described as literally "pivotal" between the liturgy of baptism and that of the eucharist. He "sealed" the former and "admitted" the new Christians into the latter—all, of course, parts of a single celebration. With the growth of the local churches, it was no longer possible for all initiations to take place under the presidency of the bishop.

In the Latin church we see the effort to maintain the bishop's personal role in initiation by reserving the "confirmation gestures" to himself, even though this meant some delay between baptism and admission to the eucharist. This applied equally to all new Christians, no matter their age. Eventually, it seems that the "acceptable" delay became, in the case of children, an "obligatory" delay ("of seven years," according to the Council of Trent). The current RC seeks to maintain the personal initiatory role for the bishop and to relate each person's initiation to the first pouring forth of the Holy Spirit on Pentecost. . . . Thus the reception of the Spirit through the ministry of the bishop shows the close bond that joins the confirmed to the church and the mandate to be witnesses of Christ among people (RC, 7).

The "close bond" is what makes possible the eucharistic communion that follows from this confirmation. (Remember, this "bond" and "mandate" are recognized primarily by the *church,* even if, due to youth or handicap, they are only dimly known to the candidate. One can imagine much of the protocol for a young crown prince being observed by family and country because his title and responsibilities are clear to them, even though the child may understand very little. Time will unfold the meaning of those realities that constituted him as heir. So, too, with the mandate of Christian initiation. It takes a lifetime to unfold the meaning of divine adoption.)

CONFIRM CHILDREN?

We remember that this question is actually a form of the larger question, "Initiate children?" Here our tradition answers a resounding "Yes." But the rationale for the answer has important implications for the present discussion.

> From earliest times, the church . . . has baptized children as well as adults. . . . Children should not be deprived of baptism, because they are baptized in the faith of the church. This faith is proclaimed for them by their parents and godparents, who represent both the local church and the whole society of saints and believers. (*Rite of Baptism for Children*, 2)

This does *not* mean that parents, godparents or the rest of the church are "substituting" for the absent faith of the child until such time as the child is able to speak for herself or himself. This very popular idea misses a central, beautiful realization that the church has about the Christian family. (That idea accounts also for the prevalent but faulty notion that confirmation is the one chance the church offers for such "personalization.")

IMMERSED IN THE CHRISTIAN HOME

When an adult who has grown up "outside" the Christian tradition comes for initiation, we work in the catechumenate to form and to test his or her capacity for Christian faith and life. In the celebration of the initiation sacraments we seek then a personal profession of faith. The case with the children of Christian parents is *quite different*. Such persons will not be growing up "outside" the church but profoundly "within" the church and, most particularly, in the church of the Christian home. The parents and godparents—the basic human environment of the child—are seen to embody the "whole society of believers." The

Christian faith, the spirit of divine adoption, will be part of the very air the child breathes. If the church did not have this vision of the Christian home, infants would not be baptized at all. But because it so regards the evangelical power of the Christian family, the church celebrates "entrance into Christ" as it welcomes the newborn children of its members. Sometimes (as in the Oriental rites and in Orthodox churches) this entrance is marked not only with the rite of baptism but also with confirmation and even with the eucharist for the infants.

UNFOLDING IDENTITY OF THE CHRISTIAN CHILD

> Children must later be formed in the faith in which they have been baptized. . . . Christian formation, which is their due, seeks to lead them gradually to learn God's plan in Christ, so that they may ultimately accept for themselves the faith in which they have been baptized. (*Rite of Baptism for Children,* 3)

In the pattern of natural growth children come to know their roots, their opportunities, their identity. Though there may be critical moments of discovery or rejection, the challenge to "accept" and develop one's true self can be said to last a lifetime. Christian faith is part of the identity of the baptized child, and it presents the same challenge. In the Roman church, the separation of the initiation sacraments has been seen as a way to mark the gradual unfolding of the Christian identity of the child.

Those who have been baptized continue on the path of Christian initiation through the sacrament of confirmation (RC, 1).

DOES THE *RITE* SUGGEST AN AGE?

> With regard to children, in the Latin church the administration of confirmation is generally postponed until about the seventh year. For pastoral reasons, however, especially to strengthen the faithful in complete obedience to Christ the Lord . . . episcopal conferences may choose an age which seems more appropriate . . . at a more mature age after appropriate formation. (RC, 11)

"Complete obedience to Christ?" Is there any member of the church who would claim to have achieved such a state? We must ask what is the *initiatory* meaning of such an idea. What does it mean as a definition of the "point of departure" for the Christian person? What does it mean in terms of a *child's* obedience? If we do not keep this focus, we can end up looking upon years of authentic discipleship as mere "probation" and upon baptism as a mere "trial membership" in the church.

LED BY FAMILY TO CONFIRMATION AND THE EUCHARIST

As we have seen, the sacraments of initiation have to do with "original" rather than with "advanced" formation as a Christian person. In the case of children this development takes place in the "formative years" and in the formative context of the family.

> The initiation of children into sacramental life is for the most part
> the responsibility and concern of Christian *parents.* They are to
> form and gradually increase a spirit of faith in the children and,
> with the help of catechetical instruction, *prepare them for* the fruitful
> reception of the sacraments of *confirmation and eucharist.* (RC, 3)

Current initiatory practices for children are particularly challenged here. We have come to see first communion and, even more so, confirmation, as the business of the parochial school or CCD program. We tend to focus on "religious education" rather than on "formation." It is true that, for some children, the years between infant baptism and immediate preparation for first communion are very lean on Christian formation. But even where such formation is strong and beautiful, we have the impression that the "real" preparation for the sacraments happens at the hands of the church professionals. Current timetables for the celebration of confirmation (in middle or late adolescence) reinforce this impression, because at that age children are less and less enveloped in the care of parents. So strong is this impression that people often argue for delaying confirmation on the grounds that "we can keep the children longer that way"—"we," meaning the professionals, and "keep them," referring to educational programs. (Here "instruction" replaces "formation," and its locus is the classroom rather than the Christian community as a network of believing persons. The result so often is that while we have "held them" longer, we have not, in fact, integrated them into church life—and confirmation simply marks the end of mandatory religion classes.) Even, and especially, in an age when families are in transition, the local church should not undercut but should strengthen and support the natural and essential formative role of Christian parents.

Enabling full but young Catholics to face the trials and challenges of adolescence remains a critical need for the church. But so, too, is the need to fortify *grown-up* Catholics in all sorts of crises and times of transitions in adulthood. This is not a matter for an initiatory experience. Rather, the process of maturing and the action of affirming one's life of faith concerns the nature and lifelong ministry of those who, by Christian initiation, are already bound together as the church of the Lord Jesus Christ.

CONCLUSIONS

The liturgical data of the postconciliar reform of the sacrament of confirmation urge that:

1. the traditional order of the sacraments of initiation be restored: baptism-confirmation-eucharist;
2. interpretations of the meaning of confirmation be harmonized with its status as the middle sacrament of initiation;
3. those baptized as infants be given Christian formation in the "formative early years" in the context of a church-strengthened family;
4. the sacraments of confirmation (with the bishop presiding) and eucharist be celebrated for and with these children as they begin to have a life "outside the family" and as they enter into the church's life as an increasingly independent and "complete" Christian, in the first few years of elementary school.

Theological Considerations

This section highlights several points of Catholic understanding of the sacraments as they apply to confirmation.

First, God is the primary host in the church's celebration of sacraments. God's gift of self is free, a gift that cannot be measured. God's gift of self is loving, nurturing, outreaching. God meets the members of the church through the divine/human activity of the sacraments, these members of the church respond in faith. No amount of activity, however worthy or holy, can equal the part of God in the celebration of the sacraments.

Second, it is precisely as members of the church that we celebrate the sacraments, not as individuals but as baptized Christians in relationship with Christ Jesus. This is important, because as soon as the mystery of God's saving presence in the church is lost from sight, the sacraments are reduced to things that are received by isolated individuals. A sacrament cannot be celebrated outside the context of faith. This context is usually the parish community. Through the parish, people come to see themselves as part of the diocesan local church, and through the bishop, as part of the church universal.

Third, the sacrament of confirmation always needs to be seen in the context of the sacraments of initiation. It is clear that in both East and West, baptism was the first sacrament for the believer, whether an adult or an infant. Confirmation in the first centuries was not seen so much as a separate sacrament but as a completion of what had already begun in baptism. Whether part of the same ceremony, as in the East, or delayed (often many years) until the bishop came to the parish, as in the West, confirmation "confirmed" what baptism began. Then the individual was led to communion with the Lord Jesus, at the table of the eucharist. Eucharist was the summit and goal of the initiation process.

This order was preserved up until the beginning of this century. It was Pope Pius X in 1910, in *Quam Singulari,* who decreed that children as early as age seven could receive their first communion. This established an irregular sequence for Christian initiation (baptism–eucharist–confirmation).

It can be argued that it does not follow that confirmation is intrinsically bound to its proper chronological relationship to baptism and eucharist. Nevertheless, the church in this sacrament wishes to recognize that in this particular action—whenever it is celebrated— there is (and has been) a constant and true manifestation of the giving of the Spirit to the one baptized in Christ Jesus. Baptism and confirmation may be, and often are, separated chronologically; they may not be separated theologically. It is interesting to note that the RCIA does not make baptism-confirmation-eucharist at the same liturgical celebration normative, but it does make the order and interrelationship of the three sacraments normative (RCIA, 206, 215, 217; also CSL, 71).

Finally, any consideration of confirmation must come originally from its theology, not its catechesis. Its theology comes from the above points: God as the primary actor in all sacramental activity, the church as the context for all sacramental activity, the sacraments of initiation as the primary locus for the sacrament of confirmation. The education and formation of candidates for this sacrament flow from these considerations.

Contrary to popular understanding, there is no difference in the personal readiness required of a candidate for confirmation compared to the readiness required for first communion. The issue of maturity needs to be seen in the context of the liturgical, theological and canonical restoration of these sacraments. The modern emphasis on witness and maturity of the candidate is a significant departure from tradition.

Canonical Considerations

The 1983 Code of Canon Law has one specific text dealing with the age for confirmation, canon 891. It reads:

> The sacrament of confirmation is to be conferred on the faithful at
> about the age of discretion unless the conference of bishops
> determines another age or there is danger of death or in the
> judgment of the minister a grave cause urges otherwise.

This statement is in agreement with the RC and the 1917 Code. However, in a slight change, the new canon uses normative language, as contrasted with the descriptive language of canon 788 of the older Code. Despite the fact that this canon has been more honored in breach than in fact, at least in the United States, the lawmakers strengthen the force of the canon by setting it in the context of the postconciliar reform of the initiatory sacraments. At this point, it is well to remember the principle of canon 842, #2. It reads:

> The sacraments of baptism, confirmation and most holy eucharist
> so converge that they are required for full Christian initiation.

This canon is not a "law" in the strict sense, for it does not mandate or prohibit any action. But it is a doctrinal clarification of what is to be presented in the law. In a certain sense, it "canonizes" the basic principle that postconciliar theologians, liturgists and canonists use as the foundation for the reform of the sacraments of initiation. Canonist Michael J. Balhoff states:

> In other words, this formulation in the new law clarifies the
> centrality of this principle and reinforces the fact that the more
> specific disciplinary norms that unite baptism, confirmation and
> eucharist must be seen in the context of this conciliar goal. To carry
> the implication one step further, the disciplinary practices that
> contribute to clarifying and maintaining the unity of the initiatory
> sacraments are seen to take precedence if there is a conflict between
> the principle of canon 842, #2 and a lesser principle such as that
> included at the end of article 11 of the *Ordo Confirmationis* (namely,
> the right of conferences of bishops to decide upon another age for
> pastoral reasons). . . . The code is clear about the rule: The
> sacraments of baptism, confirmation and eucharist must so
> converge that they express full Christian initiation. ("Age for
> Confirmation: Canonical Evidence," *Jurist* 45 [1985], 571)

In 1972, and again in 1984, the National Conference of Catholic Bishops for the United States voted in favor of maintaining the right of the local ordinary to determine the age for confirmation. It is unclear whether this is the intention of the exception allowed in canon 891, namely, to allow individual diocesan bishops to decide, against the conference deciding for all diocesan bishops in a region or nation.

Nevertheless, it seems that our committee's recommendation to implement the restored order of the sacraments of initiation in our diocese is consistent with canon law and principles upon which the law rests.

Catechetical Considerations

Catechesis, according to the *National Catechetical Directory* (NCD), is a pastoral ministry of the church through which the community of believers is encouraged to grow and mature in faith. It is a lifelong process for each individual member of the community, but it is in every form directed and oriented in some way to the catechesis of adults.

It is in and through the process of catechetics that the community of believers shares its faith, its values and its life, thus strengthening the faith life of all participants.

Children are involved in a process of catechesis because their parents desire to share their faith with them, and at some point in the child's faith development the parents see the need for a more formal process of catechesis. This usually coincides with the beginning of school.

The awareness of this relationship between the faith life of the parents and the child's development in faith has been the basis for the emphasis on parental involvement in the catechetical process.

Parents/guardians are expected to participate in ongoing programs of enrichment that nurture their own life of faith and at the same time enable them to actively participate in the development of faith in the children. They are expected and even required to attend programs at the time of the baptism of their child and also at the times of receiving the other sacraments of initiation.

The implementation of this proposal to restore the order of the sacraments of initiation by the end of the second semester of the third year of catechesis will be accomplished through a total catechetical process directed to the parish staff, to parents and then to the child in the appropriate grade.

The first thrust of the program will be directed to the parish religious education staff of the volunteer, pioneer parishes: pastor, parochial vicars, D.R.E., principal and catechists of the first three grades.

Second, the process will involve the parish adults (parents, guardians and sponsors) who are most directly responsible for the catechesis of primary children. Only after the parish staff and the parents have been adequately prepared and informed will the catechetical emphasis shift to the child.

Because catechesis must be tailored to the specific needs of the individual groups, a separate but integrated process will be directed to each group. The goals, content and method of each will be designed to accommodate these unique needs.

Staff Development

The parish religious education team will participate in a catechetical process that will enable them to grow together in their knowledge and appreciation for the sacraments of initiation in a restored order.

This process will also enable them to communicate with the parents of the primary children and to develop a catechetical program that can be integrated into the curriculum of the second and third grade programs. (See Appendix 1.) Parish staffs from neighboring parishes will be invited to participate in the staff development in order to begin the process of moving the model out into the deanery.

Parental Enrichment

The parents of children in the first half of the second year of catechesis and the first half of the third year will be involved in a parent enrichment program. Through the program, parents will be encouraged to grow in their faith and spirituality, thus enabling them to participate actively in their child's preparation for the celebration of the sacraments of reconciliation, confirmation and eucharist, which will complete the child's entrance into the community. (See Appendix 2.)

Catechesis of the Child

The principle goal for the catechetical program for the primary grade child is to support and aid the parents in their role as the primary educators of their children. It is in the family that children learn to believe what their parents' words and examples teach about God. Thus the parental participation will be the foundation on which the child's catechesis will be built.

Through the use of a curriculum that is approved and appropriate for the readiness level of the child, these children will be stimulated to grow in faith, in their ability to pray, in their appreciation for the sacraments and in their awareness of themselves as vital members of the community of faith.

There is the sad reality that in some families these foundations are lacking. However, the formal catechetical process will be a complete program. Although parental participation will be invited and expected, the children will be provided with the fullest possible catechesis.

The catechetical process for the child will begin in the first year. The sacraments of initiation will be completed by the end of their third year, and the catechetical process will continue uninterrupted until the children are fully assimilated into whatever ministerial or catechetical process is available in their particular parish when they reach their teen years.

No major changes in curriculum are necessary in order to implement the model of baptism–confirmation–eucharist as the norm for initiation in the community of faith. The curriculum for the restoration of the order of the sacraments of initiation at the primary level is outlined in Appendix 3.

The expectations for knowledge of the sacrament of confirmation are the same as the expectations currently placed on children at the time of first communion: a knowledge about the sacraments, accurate preparation according to their capacity to understand what the mystery of Christ means, the ability to receive sacraments with reverence and the desire to participate in the life of the faith community. (See Appendix 4.)

Another aspect of the total catechetical picture that must not be overlooked is the catechesis being currently directed to eighth grade students and higher. This process can continue according to the present practice. However, parents and catechists at these levels would need to be involved in a similar program of enrichment that would familiarize these young people with the sacraments of initiation.

The remaining grades, third through seventh, would continue to progress through the regular curriculum of religious education according to the present practice.

The catechetical emphasis at all levels must be congruent with the catechesis at the lower levels. Thus the restored order of the sacraments would be taught as the ordinary process of entrance into the community of faith.

Appendix 1

A staff development program would include:
1. spiritual formation of the team through liturgy and prayer;
2. overview of sacramental theology;
3. the theology and history of the sacraments of initiation;
4. study of the revised sacramental rites (baptism of children, confirmation, eucharist, RCIA);
5. overview of psychological and faith development from childhood until adulthood;
6. overview of catechetical needs of children and adults.

Appendix 2

The parental participation program would include:
1. spiritual formation through liturgy and prayer;
2. overview of history and theology of sacraments of initiation;
3. overview of the revised sacramental rites;
4. faith development of adults and children;

5. psychological and emotional development of primary age children;
6. process of catechizing children, through teachable moments;
7. integration of prayer, scripture and tradition into daily family life today.

Appendix 3

Primary curriculum for the restored order of the sacraments of initiation:

First year. Introduction to the Trinity and the wonders of creation.

Second year. Introduction to the person of Jesus and our relationship with him as a friend. An emphasis on Jesus' presence in the sacraments, with a concentration on the sacrament of reconciliation. (The reception of the sacrament of reconciliation in the second year does interrupt the order of initiatory sacraments; however, canon law requires that it be celebrated before first eucharist.)

Third year. Introduction to the Holy Spirit and the Spirit's activity through the church. The sacraments of baptism and confirmation as the sacraments of belonging to God's family, the church, with a concentration on the Pentecost experience. Concentration on the sacrament of eucharist as the continual renewal of our membership in the church and our relationship with Christ.

Appendix 4

The curriculum guidelines and knowledge requirements of the following textbook series would be appropriate as a catechetical tool to be used by the parents and catechists who have been specifically prepared for this task: *In Christ Jesus* (Benziger Publishing Company); *And These Thy Gifts* (Our Sunday Visitor); *God With Us* (William H. Sadlier, Inc.); *This Is Our Faith* (Silver Burdett and Ginn).

These textbook series are appropriate because they each develop the topic of the Spirit in the third year. This enables the parent and catechist to concentrate on the sacrament of confirmation and the building up of the church family. These series also develop the sacraments of initiation according to the restored order.

Specific Recommendations

This committee recommends that the order of the reception of the sacraments of initiation be restored to baptism-confirmation-eucharist. To implement this recommendation, it is suggested that over the next five years parishes catechize the groups related to sacramental initiation and the whole community of faith appropriately and begin this order of celebrating baptism, confirmation and eucharist.

This is the proposed sequence for the celebration of sacraments:

First Year. Catechesis for sacraments of initiation.

Second Year. In the first semester, catechesis for and reception of the sacrament of reconciliation. In the second semester, catechesis for the sacrament of confirmation. The children receive confirmation sometime between Easter Sunday of the second year and Ash Wednesday of the third year.

Third Year. In the first semester, continuing catechesis. In the second semester, catechesis for first eucharist. Reception of first eucharist takes place during the Easter season at a time determined by the parish.

For the diocese as a whole, this is the proposed plan of implementation:

First Year. Parishes would be asked to volunteer to be "pioneer" parishes within their deanery. Ideally, there would be two pioneer parishes in each deanery, one with a parochial school and one without. The parish staffs of each pioneer parish (pastor, parochial vicars, D.R.E., principal and catechists of the first three grade levels) would participate in a catechetical process to learn about the sacraments of initiation, their relationship to one another in the restored order and elements of communicating this to parents and parishioners. The staff of the diocesan religious education office would assist in the designing and carrying out of such a catechetical process. The first-grade-level students would receive their customary catechesis. Staffs from neighboring parishes would participate in this catechetical process, on a deanery level, with a view toward their parishes implementing the restored order of initiation sacraments.

Second Year. The pioneer parishes would begin the children's catechesis for reconciliation, as well as parental enrichment programs. By Lent of the second year, the children will have received reconciliation and begin catechesis for confirmation. This would be scheduled anytime between Easter Sunday of the second year and Ash Wednesday of the third year. Some other parishes in the deanery would begin their own implementation of this plan.

Third Year. The pioneer parishes would celebrate confirmation no later than Ash Wednesday. The parishes would determine the time for reception of first eucharist, during the Easter season. The rest of the parishes in the deanery would begin the implementation of this plan.

The question arises, "What about the older students?" This has to be dealt with carefully and sensitively. It is the recommendation of this committee to continue to confirm students on an annual basis until all classes of students are confirmed.

Two alternatives are also possible: 1) that large groups of candidates from several parishes be confirmed in each deanery, at the eighth-grade level; 2) that all the students from third to eighth grade in the parish be confirmed in one or two large ceremonies.

Both of these "catch-up" plans obviously demand special preparation and catechesis. They need to be presented as exceptions within the restored and implemented order of the initiation sacraments. Special attention also needs to be given to all parishioners, because this implementation of the restored order of initiation sacraments is considerably different from their own experience of receiving confirmation.

There are several liturgical notes. The liturgy of confirmation would not be in the context of the Mass. It would be frustrating and counterproductive to have the students receive confirmation from the bishop and then sit while their sponsors, parents and family members march past them to receive communion. By having confirmation celebrated outside of Mass, there is a natural longing to complete initiation, with the soon-to-happen reception of first communion.

By scheduling the reception of first communion during the Easter season of the third year, the committee members wish to give as much freedom as possible to the staffs of parishes in how the celebration proceeds. Some parishes may want to have a group first communion. Some will have children receive first communion with their families at various Sunday liturgies. Some parishes may want to offer both options. All are possible within this program design.

There will be some who will object that it is difficult enough for our bishops to do all the confirmations in the diocese as the policy stands. Each year they receive the help of several visiting bishops. Now all the confirmations are to be done within a 12-month span (and realistically there will be no confirmations celebrated during the summer months). This is a fair objection.

However, there is a way out of the dilemma. Canons 882 and 884 state:

> The ordinary minister of confirmation is the bishop; a presbyter who has this faculty by virtue of either the common law or a special concession of competent authority also confers this sacrament validly.
>
> The diocesan bishop is to administer confirmation personally or see that it is administered by another bishop, but if necessity requires he may give the faculty to administer this sacrament to one or more specified presbyters.

It would seem that these two canons were not written just to give the bishop leeway when there are many confirmations to administer, nor to weaken the ancient tradition in the Roman rite of the bishop as the ordinary minister of confirmation. The canons do foster unity in the celebration of the sacraments of initiation or, to quote canonist Michael Balhoff, they "clarify that the principle of unity of the sacraments had gained ascendancy over the principle that the bishop was the ordinary minister of confirmation." It is most desirable for a bishop to confirm. Yet to preserve the unity and order of the sacraments of initiation, delegates of the diocesan bishop, such as deans, episcopal vicars or pastors, could confirm and represent the concern of the bishop and the prayers of the diocesan church.

CHAPTER 2

Restoring
Order in
Salford, England

GEOFFREY STEEL

I N FEBRUARY 1988, as part of a project, one of my students sent a
questionnaire concerning the sacrament of confirmation to each
diocese in England and Wales. He asked: What preparation was
undertaken? Was it organized on a diocesan basis? What age were the
candidates? Was there any follow-up in the parish or diocese? The
response revealed more variation than anticipated. The greatest diver-
gence in age of candidates, upon which the bishops of England and
Wales have reached no consensus, occurs between two neighboring
dioceses.

One of these recently embarked on a radical program for completing the initiation of children baptized in infancy; radical because it
respects the normative sequence of the sacraments of initiation envisaged in the revised Roman rites, thereby overturning decades of
pastoral practice in this country. Baptized children are now confirmed
prior to receiving the eucharist.

This article describes how the change came about and outlines the
sequence of preparation and celebration. Some questions will be raised,

but assessments of the program as a whole can only be tentative because at the time of writing it has yet to complete its first cycle.

Background

The diocese of Salford comprises 208 parishes in and around Greater Manchester, northwest England. Patrick Kelly, ordained bishop of the diocese in 1984, inherited a system, widespread in England and Wales, in which confirmation was celebrated in conjunction with the bishop's visitation of the parish. Exceptions to this pattern meant that, across the diocese, confirmation took place every two to four years. The age of the confirmands ranged from nine to thirteen, though more than 50 percent were confirmed before they left primary school (from age ten to eleven).

Bishop Kelly's starting point for reflection was the renewed vision of church expressed in the documents of the Second Vatican Council and in the revised Roman rites. The underlying thrust that moved Bishop Kelly's reflection into pastoral practice came directly from the Rite of Baptism of Children.

At the heart of this rite lies the parents' profession of faith. They are "the first teachers of their child in the ways of faith," and the assembly prays that they will be "the best of teachers, bearing witness to the faith by what they say and do." The child's way into the community of faith is through the family, the domestic church.[1]

Increasingly in recent years, parishes across England and Wales have been involving parents and parish catechists in sacramental preparation programs. Formerly, such preparation was undertaken almost exclusively within the Catholic schools. It is always risky to generalize, but it is fair to say that initial hesitations about the adequacy of this development are gradually being overcome. The parish and school are now seen as supporting the parents, enabling them to share more fully in the growth in faith and discipleship of their children.

Another major factor in the bishop's reflection was the integration of Christian initiation, understood as an order taking place over a period of time within the liturgical year, the model encouraged in the

Rite of Christian Initiation of Adults (RCIA). Initiation is an entering into the mysteries of the Lord. It is a passage anchored in the liturgical year, where sacramental practice is in harmony with the message proclaimed in the ritual action of the community.

In April 1986, the diocesan religious education center issued a consultation paper: *Confirmation: A Question of Age or a Restoring of Order.* The confirming of baptized children was set squarely within the context of the normative sequence of the sacraments of initiation and was examined in the light of the norms laid down in the RCIA, particularly that of initiation as a many-phase process. Reaction was sought to the plan that the bishop proposed to implement. Some 2000 copies were circulated and 134 replies were received, mostly from groups.

The center produced *Confirmation: A Report on the Consultation* in November of the same year. Dissatisfaction with the former practice stemmed from a variety of reasons and was almost universal. The dissatisfaction had been building over a number of years, particularly among teachers, and it focused on the system as a whole, as well as on many of its individual features. At the same time, the report reflected agreement on three key issues:

- growth in faith as essential to sacramental formation;
- the need for stronger links between parish, family and school in order to foster the formation of the individual child;
- formation in a variety of lay ministries as a prime concern.

There was no consensus on the ideal age or grade of the candidates. At this point, a consensus on the issue did not seem needed.

Although in November 1986 Bishop Kelly intended that no major change in the celebration of confirmation would be introduced before 1988, consultation with the Congregation for Divine Worship in 1987 accelerated development. In conversation with the Cardinal Prefect during the course of an *ad limina* visit, the bishop asked how the Congregation would react to the following:

- the systematic restoring of the order of the sacraments of initiation for children baptized in infancy;

- the annual celebration of confirmation in every parish at Pentecost, with parish clergy as ministers.

Reactions were favorable. The appropriate congregations were kept informed, and the diocese will prepare a full report in consultation with the bishops' conference.

The New Plan

We now move on to the arrangements recently adopted in the diocese for completing the initiation of children baptized in infancy. These were launched by means of a pastoral letter in July 1987 and through the regular study days for the clergy, at which the bishop spoke and fielded questions.[2] In addition, the religious education center provided guidelines for establishing parish teams, and staff from the center worked in deaneries with teachers, parish coordinators and other groups.[3]

The program lasts one and a half liturgical years (about 17 months) and was inaugurated in Advent 1987. The phasing in of the new plan was achieved by offering confirmation at Pentecost 1988 to all children who would have received the eucharist by then. The phasing in also involved postponing for one year the reception of the eucharist by some children. Below is given an outline of the plan as it will normally operate:

OUTLINE:

ADVENT.   Preparation begins at this stage chiefly for parents.

THE PRESENTATION OF THE LORD.   In the course of a liturgy of the word in each parish on or around this feast, candidates are presented by their parents and sponsors.

MASS OF CHRISM (HOLY THURSDAY).   Parents, catechists, sponsors and parish coordinators are invited to attend the Mass of Chrism held in the cathedral.

PENTECOST.   Confirmation takes place in each parish. The sacrament is ministered by the pastor and other local clergy, with the bishop presiding in the cathedral parish. The context for the sacrament is a liturgy of the word, and the celebration culminates in the solemn praying of the "Our Father." The children are seven years old.

ADVENT.   In their parishes, confirmed children celebrate the sacrament of penance sometime during this season.[4]

EASTER.   With their families, the children receive the eucharist at a Mass of parental choice. The children are eight years old. Some weeks after, there is a eucharistic celebration in each parish for all the children who recently completed their Christian initiation.[5]

PREPARATION

At this point, it will be helpful to give some indication of the scope of the preparation. Parents, Roman Catholic schools and catechists are all involved. In each parish the program is coordinated by a layperson. Parish catechists (one adult to every four children is seen as the norm) exercise a role of sharing faith, rather than one of formal religious instruction and so complement rather than usurp the part played by teachers in the parish school. In school the plan covers two academic years, and it is hoped that there might be less compartmentalizing of sacramental preparation and a greater involvement of the school as a whole in Christian initiation. As well as a sponsor, each child is given a "prayer sponsor," usually an elderly or housebound parishioner who prays for the child throughout the period of preparation.[6] Material for use during the program has been provided by the diocesan religious education center to supplement the teaching materials already in use. This is offered as a guideline, and parishes are free to adapt according to their own needs.

DIFFICULTIES WITH THE LAUNCH

Inevitably, there were teething difficulties. Dissatisfaction over consultation procedures was a major factor. Before the plan was launched, there was strong opposition. Some parents felt that the change had been sprung on them. Even though the favorable response to the consultation paper may have been statistically high, a large number of parents had not studied it thoroughly (for whatever reason). During the phasing in of the plan, a sizable number of children had their reception of the eucharist delayed by one year so that they could be confirmed beforehand. This delay of first communion was not popular with some parents. But perhaps the greatest source of difficulty was that parents simply did not see the reasons for the whole change of pastoral policy.

Some school administrators and faculty members opposed the plan, perhaps fearful of a weakening in the sacramental formation of the children and aware of a certain lack of commitment on the part of some parents.

Some clergy felt that they had been pushed into the change of policy following the bishop's meeting with the Congregation for Divine Worship. Others expressed the fear that the new plan would not be supported by some of their colleagues and would suffer accordingly. Still others were concerned that the plan made no provision for adolescents. It was also said that some clergy did not understand the reason for placing confirmation before reception of the eucharist.

Reflecting on these reactions, Bishop Kelly himself later admitted: "With hindsight, perhaps consultation could have been broader."[7]

THE RESULTS SO FAR

The Salford plan is now well under way, and the first group received the sacrament of confirmation on Pentecost 1988, the sacrament of penance in Advent of 1988 and eucharist on Easter 1989. So far it seems to be working, at least to me as an outsider.

My information has not been gathered systematically, nor can I guarantee that the opinions expressed to me have been representative. But the impression I have received is that in parishes where the scheme was welcomed wholeheartedly, everyone is well pleased. In others, where it was adopted with reservation or reluctance, enthusiasm is growing (or at least skepticism is diminishing), and active involvement in many other aspects of parish life is on the increase. Over the diocese as a whole, acceptance and enthusiasm seem to be high. If they are not 100 percent, this is hardly a new phenomenon.[8] Periodically, the

Catholic press contains a rumble of discontent, but this would seem to be both localized and unrepresentative. It is interesting to note, now that the plan is in effect, that its critics tend to be from outside the diocese.

Inevitably, in the first year under the new plan, some parents chose to take their children to a neighboring diocese for confirmation by a bishop. This, of course, is regrettable, and some of Salford's critics have taken it as a sign of the plan's failure. I do not believe such inference to be justified. Statistics of emigration are not available to me, but even if as many as 300 children were taken elsewhere by disgruntled parents, we must remember that the number confirmed in 1988 was 17,000. This is an opt-out rate of 1.74 percent—hardly cause for alarm.

Specific Questions

Having outlined the initiative, I would now like to consider some of its aspects in more detail.

PARENTAL INVOLVEMENT

As with previous sacramental programs, the degree of commitment required of parents is high. Meetings, liturgies, prayer and study in the home—all this demands a great deal from parents. But then, so too does the baptism of a child. Parents are repeatedly questioned in the Rite of Baptism of Children about their awareness and acceptance of their responsibility. They are "the first teachers of their child in the ways of faith." Therefore, parental responsibility and involvement during the final stages of preparation of their child for a sacrament cannot be side-stepped.

But what of parents who simply are not committed to the continued formation of their baptized child? As with infant baptism, it is not a question of refusal but of delay in order to give time for such parents to be helped to understand and accept the responsibility of Christian parenthood envisaged in the liturgy of the church. One particular advantage of the new Salford approach is that, with the plan in effect each year, it is possible to suggest to such parents that they wait a year. Formerly, they may have had to wait four years, until the bishop's next visitation. The pastor is not faced with the dilemma of either needing to persuade them not to bother at all or of accepting their child knowing full well that the home background in no way fosters continued growth in faith and discipleship. Perhaps with the Salford plan, doors are being kept open rather than being closed in people's faces.[9]

RITE OF PRESENTATION

A rite of presentation was prepared by the religious education center. Parishes were free to adapt it to their own needs. It was suggested, both by the bishop and the center, that the rite be held outside of Mass, because the candidates themselves would not be receiving the eucharist.[10]

MASS OF CHRISM

This is held in the cathedral on Holy Thursday morning. Parents, catechists, parish coordinators and sponsors of the children who will be confirmed at Pentecost with chrism consecrated by the bishop are invited to participate. It might be thought that holding the Mass of Chrism on a weekday morning does not make it easy for lay people to attend. Yet because of the popularity of this Mass in the diocese of Salford, the cathedral is, in fact, packed, and parishes are restricted to sending four representatives.

At this year's Mass of Chrism, the first under the new plan, four flagons of chrism were presented by parish coordinators, and the bishop read a document delegating clergy to confirm. A copy of the letter of delegation was given to two people from each parish who read it at the evening Mass of the Lord's Supper.[11]

CONFIRMATION

There was said to have been some anxiety over confirming outside Mass. This concern arose probably for two reasons.

The first was current pastoral practice in England, where confirmation takes place during Mass. But, of course, those candidates have already received the eucharist, perhaps years earlier.

The Introduction to the Rite of Confirmation, 13, envisages that confirmation be celebrated outside Mass if the candidates have not yet received the eucharist and are not to do so at the confirmation liturgy.[12]

In advocating confirmation outside Mass, Bishop Kelly has drawn attention to the pastoral situation of many families, where a parent—or perhaps both—is unable for whatever reason to receive the eucharist. At least on this occasion they are not publicly embarrassed.

The second reason for the concern about confirmation outside Mass is, I believe, awareness of the possibility that if the liturgy does not incorporate the eucharist, then some parents and children might not even participate in the eucharist on Pentecost. This consideration can be appreciated, but if it is actually the case, then perhaps the plan is not being implemented so well as it might be. Commitment to Sunday eucharist must be one of the criteria for which the parents of candidates for confirmation and the candidates themselves are held responsible.

Some promotion of the confirmation liturgy in the parish may well be needed, lest the celebration be seen as being solely for the children and their families. (In future years this could be a fairly small number in some places.) A great deal will depend on the involvement of the whole parish in the complete initiatory process.

RECEPTION OF FIRST COMMUNION

The plan completes its first cycle in 1989. The children receive first communion with their families and sponsors, either at the Vigil or at one of the Masses on Easter Day itself. Two problems have already been expressed about this.

First, it is said that this marks a break with the practice of children receiving first communion as a group at a special Mass. In fact, this custom is no longer as widespread in England as it once was. In recent years the practice of children receiving first communion in smaller groups at a Sunday parish Mass during the season of Easter has grown considerably.[13]

As the culmination of Christian initiation, having the children receive first communion at Easter has a great deal to commend it. There is certainly no need to add artificial ceremonial. A person, whether adult or child, receives first communion on this day precisely because it is Easter. Full sacramental initiation (and/or reception into full communion) at the Great Vigil, the baptism of infants at one of the Masses on Easter Day and especially the renewal of baptismal promises and sprinkling with water—all this provides an excellent symbolic and catechetical context for children receiving first eucharist.

What is required, therefore, is not the retention of secondary ceremonial customs surrounding first communion. Far more important is the formation of the whole parish in the liturgies of the Sacred Triduum together with renewed emphasis on their worthy celebration, especially the Great Vigil and Masses on Easter Day.[14]

In parishes where the plan has been implemented wholeheartedly and where it is already bearing much fruit in the quality of parish life, one would expect that the degree of parental involvement in the process as a whole will more than compensate for the absence of a separate first communion Mass where this had been the custom.

Second, some concern about first communion at Easter may center on the fact that the two weeks from Passion Sunday to the Second Sunday of Easter are usually a school holiday. Certainly it is not demanding too much to expect that families celebrate Easter even if the children are not attending school at that time. (If it *is* demanding too much of some families, then, once again, perhaps the preparation work with parents needs to be strengthened.) But what of families who go off on holiday at this time of year? Is it really optimum, or even appropriate, for a child to receive first communion not in the local parish but in *any* church, a church that simply happens to be in the family's holiday location?

There is also the question of the sponsors: As integral participants in the child's initiation, what happens when the family goes away at Easter? It seems odd that the sponsor might be absent from the culmination of the child's initiation. It will be important to monitor this potential problem during the first few years of the Salford plan.

FOLLOW-UP CELEBRATION

If this is held too close to Easter Day, there may be the temptation for parents to leave their child's first communion until this celebration involving all the children of the parish who recently were to have received first communion, for it certainly will be a jolly affair. One suggestion has been to make the Solemnity of the Body and Blood of Christ the occasion for this celebration.

THE ROLE OF THE BISHOP

Does the Salford plan restore order to the sacraments of initiation at the expense of the involvement of the bishop? This is a value retained in the West, at least for one of the sacraments, namely confirmation. Is such reduction in his involvement as the Salford plan requires a price worth paying for the restoration of the sequence of the sacraments of initiation?

The norms for initiation in the Roman Catholic church are set out in the Rite of Christian Initiation of Adults (RCIA). One must recognize that most adult candidates will not have a bishop presiding at the sacraments of initiation. At the same time, one hopes that at least one of the other steps of the RCIA will be presided over by the bishop, particularly the rite of election. In Salford, the bishop presides in the cathedral over the confirmation of the children who belong to that parish. In terms of a diocesan celebration, he presides at the Mass of Chrism, to which parents, catechists, sponsors and parish coordinators are invited. But this does not involve the children. The idea of holding the follow-up celebration Mass for the fully initiated children in the cathedral had been suggested, but it is not being pursued at present.[15]

For his part, Bishop Kelly sees his main task as being to foster the unity of parishes with each other. He has argued that the bishop moving around the diocese to minister the sacrament of confirmation has not given individual parishes a sense of being linked through the bishop with other parishes throughout the diocese. In contrast, the new plan is able to promote a stronger sense of diocesan unity because all parishes are celebrating the same sacraments at the same time. Another positive result of detaching confirmation from episcopal visitation is that the visit can now encompass more aspects of parish life. A particular feature being emphasized in Salford is the anointing of sick, elderly parishioners at a common celebration.

All the same, it would seem both important and desirable that Salford work to develop ways of involving the bishop more directly in the initiation of the children of the whole diocese. By extending to presbyters the ministry of confirming, the church has clearly placed restoring the normative sequence of the sacraments of initiation as a higher value than episcopal presiding for confirmation. Nevertheless, the present Salford arrangements could be seen as making less provision for the bishop's direct involvement in initiation than is appropriate.

ADOLESCENTS

What of the liturgical-sacramental needs of adolescents? These lie outside the scope of the Salford arrangements concerning the sacraments of initiation, and so the absence of any such provision should not be a point of criticism of the plan itself. Nevertheless, there is real lack of liturgical rites of passage for those in adolescence. The ritual and symbolism of confirmation were never intended to meet their needs, and I believe that we are wrong in trying to force them to do so.

There is more than one question here: At what age does one fix a "rite for adolescents"? In a group of 16-year-old teens, there will be a fairly wide range of maturity, sense of commitment and experience. Also, is a "check-that-one-off" liturgy likely to meet their needs? I think not, not even a liturgy of confirmation. Adolescence is a *period*, not a moment, and liturgical provision must respect this. Perhaps the need is for a "phased rite," for a repeatable liturgy or the celebration of several moments of adolescence in different contexts: school, family, parish, diocese.

Perhaps Salford could once again take the lead and give serious consideration to ways of celebrating in liturgy the passage of adolescents into adulthood. Such liturgies would provide an alternative for those in other dioceses who, recognizing the need for some sort of rite of adult commitment, are keen to retain confirmation as a sacrament for teenagers.

Currently, the diocese is beginning to make some provision for teenagers leaving secondary school (age 15–16) through parish-based preparation for a diocesan celebration in the cathedral. This should be seen in conjunction with the continuing liturgical formation of children who have completed their initiation.

In October 1988, the diocese launched a program of formation in the sacrament of penance. Prior to completing their sacramental initiation, the children are introduced to the sacrament of penance in the context of Rite II, the communal celebration with individual confession and absolution. Having completed their initiation at age eight or nine, the children continue to experience Rite II. There is particular emphasis on the joint responsibility of sharing in the eucharist and of reconciliation.

Without dropping Rite II the program then prepares the children for Rite I for individual penitents. Here, emphasis is placed on inner disposition and the effects of sin. At ages ten and eleven the children continue to experience both rites and are encouraged to be more aware of increased responsibility for their own actions and so for acts of reconciliation.[16]

This still leaves the need to provide something specifically for teenagers, but this most recent development in Salford is certainly an imaginative step in the right direction.

Criticism

With its new arrangements, Salford comes closer than any other diocese in England and Wales to respecting both the liturgical norms and the law of the church as regards the sacraments of initiation. At the beginning of this article I stated that any assessment of the Salford program at this early stage is tentative. There are, however, two features that need to be questioned. Whether the plan is able to adapt itself accordingly will be, I believe, a significant measure of its lasting value.

DELAYED RECEPTION OF THE EUCHARIST

The first point of criticism concerns the systematic delay between confirmation and reception of the eucharist. The Introduction to the Rite of Confirmation, 13, states:

> Confirmation takes place as a rule within Mass in order that the
> fundamental connection of this sacrament with all of Christian
> initiation may stand out in clearer light. Christian initiation reaches
> its culmination in the communion of the body and blood of Christ.
> The newly confirmed therefore participate in the eucharist, which
> completes their Christian initiation.[17]

In the Salford scheme, however, confirmation takes place in
principle and "as a rule" *outside* Mass. Thus the norm given in the first
paragraph of section 13 of the Introduction is ignored, and practice is
based instead upon the exception mentioned in the second paragraph:

> If the candidates for confirmation are children who have not
> received the eucharist and are not being admitted to first
> communion at this liturgical celebration or if there are other special
> circumstances, confirmation should be celebrated outside Mass.[18]

Looking at the Rite of Confirmation, one can see that, celebrated
outside of Mass, it does not itself express the fundamental connection
between confirmation and the eucharist requested by the Second
Vatican Council.[19] Nor does it express the fact that initiation culminates
in communion.

The Salford plan manifests the fact that initiation is a process. But
is this not expressed at the expense of artificially separating confirmation from the reception of the eucharist? What is the rationale for
delaying communion once a child has been confirmed? This would be
unacceptable practice in the initiation of adults and of children who
have reached catechetical age.[20] In the preparation of uncatechised
adults for confirmation and the eucharist.[21] Why, then, is the delay
acceptable when the candidates are children who have already been
baptized?[22] If adult and child candidates for initiation and baptized but
uncatechized adults are not given further catechesis between confirmation and reception of the eucharist, why must baptized children be
given some? Though the *methods* of catechesis may differ, the *principle* of
formation in faith and discipleship through liturgy are the same,
regardless of the age of the candidate.

It would seem from the liturgical books that separating the sacraments of initiation needs to be justified just as much as does ignoring the normative and proper sequence.[23] The delay of communion following confirmation is, I believe, a significant weakness of the Salford program. The norm expressed in the Introduction to the Rite of Confirmation, 13, merits closer attention.

The Sacrament of Penance

The second aspect of the plan on which I would like to focus is reconciliation. Children of the diocese of Salford approach this sacrament having been confirmed and before receiving the eucharist. This is not the place to argue against penance before first eucharist except to note that we are inconsistent in our requirements.

Prior to reception into full communion, a baptized person makes a confession of sins "according to his or her own conscience."[24] It is not *required*. Nor is it required when an uncatechized Roman Catholic adult is preparing for confirmation and eucharist. Lenten preparation for the sacrament of penance is mentioned, but a confession of sins before the completion of initiation is not indicated.[25] In contrast, when initiating children who have reached catechetical age, it is envisaged that lenten penitential services (scrutinies) are "a proper occasion for baptized children of catechetical age to celebrate the sacrament of penance for the first time."[26] It is envisaged that these same children "may be completing their Christian initiation in the sacraments of confirmation and the eucharist" at the celebration where the other children are to be fully initiated.[27] Why this inconsistency?

It is unfortunate, then, that, having restored the normative sequence of the sacraments of initiation for children baptized in infancy, the Salford plan has built into it two features that work against the integrity of those three sacraments and undermine the intimate link between confirmation and eucharist, namely, the time gap and the sacrament of penance.[28]

Leaving aside its intrusion before communion, for this is not peculiar to Salford and the diocese is to be admired for seeking to develop a pattern of post-initiatory formation in the sacrament, there is a second criticism connected with the sacrament of penance in the Salford program, namely, the place in the liturgical year of the children's introduction to it: Advent. This seems at odds with the concern to have the various sacramental celebrations coordinated with the mysteries highlighted in the liturgical year. Whatever its history, the season of Advent is no longer seen as a second cousin to Lent. It is described in the *General Norms for the Liturgical Year and the Calendar* as "a period for devout and joyful expectation."[29] The commentary by the consilium appended to the norms states that it is no longer to be considered as a penitential season.[30] Moreover, *not* to celebrate the sacrament of penance for the first time during Lent would seem to be a serious drawback in the Salford plan, occasioned, one suspects, by having to situate penance before communion and yet wanting sufficient time for catechesis between each sacrament.[31]

The two flaws to which I have drawn attention here detract, I believe, from the success with which the Salford plan respects initiation as an order of rites and periods in harmony with the liturgical year.

Concluding Remarks

This is the plan for completing the initiation of children baptized in infancy recently inaugurated in the diocese of Salford. There is much to commend, and other dioceses would do well to give it serious consideration. As suggested at the outset, it will need to be in operation for some years before a valuable and reasonably objective assessment can be made. Meanwhile, parishes will, I am sure, soon find it influencing the way in which couples prepare for marriage and parents prepare for the baptism of their children. It could also exercise an influence upon the implementation and operation of the RCIA, as well as being further influenced by the adult catechumenate in return.

Some may wish that Salford had approached the whole question from a different starting point, restoring confirmation to infant baptism and concentrating on forming children for the culmination of initiation in communion. This may not have been possible, of course, and it has not been my purpose here to propose a wholly different plan.

For now, how one assesses the present initiative will, I suspect, largely depend upon the value one places upon the restoration of the order of the sacraments of initiation: If *sequence* is one's sole concern, then delaying first communion after confirmation may not pose a difficulty. If, however, one values the sequence of the three sacraments in the context of other norms for initiation, then one should be concerned both about separating the reception of communion from confirmation and about the placement of the introduction to the sacrament of penance. Ultimately, is the great value of the Salford initiative impaired by too much weight being placed on a particular catechetical method at the expense of liturgical principle?

Notes

1. My presentation of Bishop Kelly's own reflection is based on three cassette tapes: Patrick Kelly, "Sacraments of Initiation," and "Sacraments of Initiation: Response to Questions" (Diocese of Salford Religious Education Center, 5 Gerald Road, Salford M6 6DL). The first is the bishop's address to the clergy and the second is his response to questions raised in deanery discussions. The third cassette is an interview the bishop gave to Martin Kershaw, to whom I am grateful, who sent the questionnaire on the sacrament of confirmation to the dioceses of England and Wales. In addition, a private conversation with Bishop Kelly on November 8, 1988, enabled me to clarify the presentation in some detail.

2. Two study days are held each year, and, in retrospect, one can see how the whole area of faith commitment had been an underlying concern for some time.

3. It was recommended that the program coordinator in each parish be a nonordained rather than an ordained person.

4. It was envisaged that the children's first experience of the sacrament of penance will be in the context of Rite II, the communal celebration with individual confession and absolution. This question is discussed below. My understanding is that Bishop Kelly was required to place the sacrament of penance before first communion.

5. I am uncertain to what extent, if any, the structure of the Salford plan matches that of the archdiocese of Brisbane, Australia: "Since 1974 . . . confirmation is administered in most parishes on Pentecost Sunday by the parochial pastor. The bishops also confirm on other occasions." Gerard Austin, *Anointing with the Spirit— The Rite of Confirmation: The Use of Oil and Chrism,* Studies in the Reformed Rites of the Catholic Church III (New York: Pueblo, 1985), 63, note 38. The Brisbane practice is also referred to in *Confirmation: A Report on the Consultation,* 28. For another approach, see Richard P. Moudry, "The Initiation of Children: The Path One Parish Took," *Catechumenate: A Journal of Christian Initiation* (July 1987), 27–33. In this parish, children baptized in infancy are confirmed by the bishop and receive the eucharist for the first time in the one liturgy. See also Terri McKenzie and Michael J. Savelesky, "Confirmation with First Communion? It Works!" *Chicago Catechumenate* (May 1986), 16–23.

6. In preparation programs for the reception of the eucharist and for confirmation, the idea of a "prayer sponsor" had already proved popular and fruitful in many parishes across a number of dioceses.

7. *Universe* (April 15, 1988), 12-13.

8. North American readers should bear in mind that many parishes in England and Wales are only beginning to implement the RCIA and to discover its riches and vision. I suspect that whether a parish did or did not already have experience of the adult catechumenate would have influenced its approach to the new Salford plan.

9. Such is Bishop Kelly's own hope. It will be interesting after five or more years of the carrying out the plan to research the pastoral practice with reluctant or uncommitted parents of candidates.

10. In 1988, because of the large number of candidates occasioned by the phasing in of the new plan, many parishes held several rites of presentation. I am told that rites of presentation were held within Mass for those candidates who had already received the eucharist. It seemed pointless to pretend otherwise. Also, this was the first major rite of the new plan and thus the first real exposure to it of the parish as a whole. Where the rite was celebrated outside of Mass, some parents were unhappy. In future years, when the candidates will not already have received the eucharist and when the plan is more familiar, holding the rite of presentation outside Mass will be more feasible.

11. There is a novel practice on the increase in England and Wales, where the oils consecrated in the Chrism Mass are brought into a parish in solemn procession at the Evening Mass of the Lord's Supper on Holy Thursday. It would seem necessary to accompany this rite with some explanation, and this may considerably overload and detract from the already-rich symbolism of the occasion. With regard to reading the bishop's delegation of local clergy to confirm, at one level it makes sense to do this when the oils are received into the parish. At the same time, delegation is not needed for the confirmation of candidates initiated or received into full communion at the Easter Vigil. Would it not be better to read the delegation when it is actually needed, namely at Pentecost, when the confirmation is of children already baptized? In 1988 in Salford, it was suggested that the procession of oils and the reading of the bishop's mandate be integrated with the General Intercessions. This fails to respect the nature and function of these prayers and will, no doubt, restrict their proper scope.

12. The norm envisaged in the Introduction to the Rite of Confirmation, 13, is discussed below. I understand that in 1988 again, because of the large numbers, most parishes celebrated several confirmation liturgies within Masses for those who had already received the eucharist. Once the phasing in of the new plan is complete, one confirmation liturgy, celebrated with a liturgy of the word, will probably suffice for each parish, as originally proposed.

13. I am grateful to my colleague Reverend Hugh Preston, SDB, for drawing my attention to the extent of this development.

14. Some care may also be needed lest the occasion of confirmation overshadow that of first eucharist, though the time lapse between the two events may well mean that this possible difficulty will not arise.

15. Such a celebration is envisaged in the RCIA, 241. (All references to the RCIA are to the definitive edition published for England and Wales.) However, there are practical difficulties facing a diocesan celebration involving all the children: Each year, some 5000 will complete their initiation. With parents and brothers and sisters, this would necessitate either holding perhaps as many as ten Masses in the cathedral, or else moving into a sports stadium for the occasion. Neither option seems desirable. The same would apply to a diocesan celebration of the rite of presentation.

16. These details are taken from the proposals sent out from the diocesan religious education center, October 24, 1988.

17. See the International Committee on English in the Liturgy (ICEL), ed., *Documents on the Liturgy 1963–1979: Conciliar, Papal, and Curial Texts* (Collegeville, Minnesota: The Liturgical Press, 1982), #2522.

18. Ibid.

19. See the Constitution on the Sacred Liturgy (CSL), 71.

20. See RCIA, 208, 281.

21. Ibid., 385; Introduction, Rite of Confirmation, 11.

22. It should be noted that "The Initiation of Children Who Have Reached Catechetical Age" envisages that baptized children of the catechetical group will be confirmed by a presbyter and that they receive the eucharist in the same liturgy of initiation (RCIA, 284). The Salford plan contrasts with that described by Moudry and by McKenzie and Savelesky, where children are both confirmed and receive communion for the first time in the one liturgy. (See note 5.)

23. For further rationale on this point, see Aidan Kavanagh, *Confirmation: Origins and Reform* (New York: Pueblo, 1988), 87–88, 97–99.

24. RCIA, 395.

25. Ibid., 384.

26. Ibid., 269, and see 279.

27. Ibid., 284.

28. The anomaly of the sacrament of penance in this location was mentioned in *Confirmation: A Report on the Consultation,* 28, where it was tentatively suggested that this sacrament might be prepared for and celebrated at some time during adolescence. The recent program of post-initiation formation in the sacrament of penance could well be developed further in this area. As mentioned earlier, my understanding is that Bishop Kelly was required to place the sacrament of penance before reception of the eucharist.

29. CSL, *General Norms for the Liturgical Year and the Calendar,* 39; ICEL, *Documents,* #3805.

30. See Consilium, "Commentarium in annum liturgicum instauratum," in Sacra Congregatio Ritum, *Calendarium Romanum* 61 (Rome: Vatican Polyglot Press, 1969): "In instauratione liturgica, Adventus suum temporis spatium servat, nempe quattuor hebdomadarum, attamen non amplius habetur tantum ut tempus paenitentiale; quinimmo tempus est laetae expectationis."

31. At the same time, the Salford arrangements may help to dilute an understanding of the sacrament of penance as being required automatically and immediately before (first) communion.

CHAPTER 3

Confirmation Guidelines for the Archdiocese of St. Paul and Minneapolis

JOHN R. ROACH
AND WILLIAM H. BULLOCK

A S A SACRAMENT of initiation, confirmation is intimately related to baptism and the eucharist. Christians are reborn in baptism, strengthened by confirmation and sustained by the eucharist. Specifically, in confirmation they are signed with the gift of the Spirit and become more perfect images of their Lord. They are so marked with the character or seal of the Lord that the sacrament of confirmation cannot be repeated (Rite of Confirmation [RC], 2). Confirmation renews and strengthens the Christian's baptismal call to bear witness to Christ before the world and to work eagerly for the building up of his body, the church.

Confirmation emphasizes the transformation of life by the outpouring of the Holy Spirit. Confirmed Christians claim as fully their own the new life into which they were initiated at baptism. The church expresses its continued support and concern for the spiritual growth of those who are confirmed and at the same time looks to them to assist others to grow and mature in the Christian life (*National Catechetical Directory* [NCD], 118).

Through a long and complicated evolution, the celebration of confirmation of children has become separated from the celebration of the other sacraments of initiation. This practice has obscured the intimate relationship of the sacraments of baptism, confirmation and eucharist. The reform of the liturgical rites accomplished by Pope Paul VI makes clear again that confirmation is a sacrament of Christian initiation, intimately connected to baptism and eucharist.

A. Preparation for Confirmation

Preparation for confirmation, like baptism, takes place within the parish community. The parish is the faith community into whose life of worship and prayer those to be confirmed will be more fully initiated. It also embodies the message to which they are to respond and gives witness in service to the faith they profess.

The initiation of children into the sacramental life is for the most part the responsibility and concern of Christian parents. They are to form and gradually increase a spirit of faith in their children and, with the help of catechetical institutions, prepare them for the fruitful reception of confirmation and first communion (RC, 3).

Preparation for confirmation involves the coordinated efforts of:

- A Planning Team: Each parish should organize a planning team, according to its own resources, to assist parents in their role of preparing their children for confirmation and to coordinate and facilitate preparation for confirmation, the celebration of the sacrament and ongoing catechesis for and involvement of those about to be confirmed in the community's life and ministry.
- Parents: As noted already, parents play a critically important role in preparing their children for confirmation. They should be totally involved in the planning for and experience of catechesis, for this will help them to renew and strengthen their own faith, and enable them to set an example for their children.
- Sponsors: Their witness to a life of faith and their involvement in the catechesis for confirmation is supportive both to those who are to be confirmed and to their parents.

- The Parish Community: The whole parish community should enter into the preparation for the celebration of the sacrament of confirmation. It should pray for and with the candidates and their families, enter with them into the ongoing conversion to which all are called, witness to the living of the Christian life by living out the fruits of the Holy Spirit and assist wherever possible in catechesis.
- Catechists: The catechists nurture faith development through personal interaction, instruction, group sessions, a prayerful environment, a strong sense of trust and their own sense of mission.

B. THE PARTICIPANTS IN THE CELEBRATION OF THE SACRAMENT OF CONFIRMATION

THE RECIPIENT OF CONFIRMATION. Based on the original intent of the sacrament as chrismation or sealing of baptism (NCD, 118), the one who presides over the celebration of baptism (usually the bishop) would in the same ceremony also confirm the newly baptized, at whatever age. Catechesis would be done with the parents; the children would receive their formation after the reception of the sacrament. There would be a parallel here to the present practice of the church with regard to infant baptism.

The Code of Canon Law uses the age of discretion as a reference for determining when confirmation is to be conferred:

> The sacrament of confirmation is to be conferred on the faithful around the age of discretion, unless the episcopal conference determines some other age, or unless there is present danger of death or some other grave cause which in the judgment of the minister persuades otherwise. (Canon 891)

The Rite of Confirmation likewise refers to the age of discretion as the appropriate age for the celebration of the sacrament: "With regard to children, in the Latin church the administration of confirmation is generally postponed until the seventh year" (11).

The term "age of discretion" is an often quoted and little understood term. It probably identifies the approximate age when most children move from objective to subjective responsibility in moral judgments. This means that a youngster will judge the seriousness of an action solely on the basis of the material consequences, while an older child will judge on the basis of the intention of the one performing the action. At the same time, the seven- to eight-year-old child is moving from heteronomy ("They made me do it.") to autonomy ("I am responsible."). [Jean] Piaget relates this to the way children view rules—as coming solely from adult authority, or as being tools for cooperation and the good of the group (cf. Ronald Duska and Mariellen Whelan, *Moral Development: A Guide to Piaget and Kohlberg* [New York: Paulist Press, 1975], 15–27). Generally, it is held that a child reaches the age of discretion about the "seventh year more or less," for it is at this age that the child begins to reason (*General Cathechetical Directory* [GCD], 98, 1).

The ordering of the sacraments in both the Code and the ritual has significance. Confirmation is seen as a continuation on the path of Christian initiation which begins at baptism and culminates in first holy communion. This ordering of the sacraments is faithful to that set down by Pope Paul VI in the Apostolic Constitution on the Sacrament of Confirmation (Cf. *The Rites of the Catholic Church as Revised by the Second Vatican Ecumenical Council and Published by Authority of Pope Paul VI,* English translation prepared by the International Commission on English in the Liturgy [New York: Pueblo Publishing Co., 1976], 292): "Finally, confirmation is so closely linked with the holy eucharist that the faithful, after being signed by holy baptism and confirmation, are incorporated fully into the body of Christ by participation in the eucharist." A fairly strict adherence to the age of discretion as the appropriate age for the celebration of the sacrament of confirmation would be required to follow the ordering of the sacraments of initiation set forth in the Code and the ritual. But, it must be recalled, this is in service to a deeper reality, that is, expressing in the clearest manner possible the rich mystery of Christian initiation.

The Rite of Confirmation is cognizant of the current practice of postponing confirmation until the early—or in some cases, the later—teens: "For pastoral reasons, however, especially to strengthen the faithful in complete obedience to Christ the Lord and in loyal testimony to him, episcopal conferences may choose an age which seems more appropriate, so that the sacrament is given at a more mature age after appropriate formation" (11). This cognizance derives from the pastoral practice surrounding confirmation, a practice that is relatively recent. It is one of the outcomes of the urging by Pope Pius X that children begin communicating at the age of seven. As a consequence, confirmation began to be celebrated "out of order," that is, after first communion. The justification for this was that a child should not be denied communion simply because the bishop was not available to confirm the child by age seven.

The pastoral practice of conferring confirmation at a later age sees confirmation as completing the experience of Christian initiation by making a personal commitment to Christ and the church. Celebrating the sacrament at a later age provides the candidate with the opportunity to receive better catechesis, thus paving the way for informed personal commitment.

The key elements of this informed catechesis are service and witness, for the celebration of the sacrament calls and challenges the candidate to model Jesus' life more fully. "The experience of Christian community leads naturally to service. Christ gives his people different gifts not only for themselves but for others. Each must serve the other for the good of all" (*To Teach as Jesus Did,* 28). "Catechesis seeks to move people to live justly, mercifully, and peacefully as individuals, to act as the leaven of the gospel in family, school, work, social and civic life, and to work for appropriate social change" (NCD, 170).

There are some dangers involved in uncritically adopting the latter view. It can lead to a belief that confirmation is the source of Christian commitment. Such a view forgets that "confirmation is a confirmation of the baptismal gift; Holy Communion continually renews and sustains it" (G. W. H. Lampe, *The Seal of the Spirit,* Second Edition [London: Alcuin Club, 1967], xxix, as quoted in William B. Bausch, *A New Look at the Sacraments,* Revised Edition [Mystic, Connecticut: Twenty-Third Publications, 1983, 1977], 108). It can also lead to the thought pattern that somehow confirmation replaces baptism, instead of ratifying it. Bausch observes that it is precisely because of such dangers that some, especially liturgists, have urged that the unity of the rite of Christian initiation be restored, either by celebrating the three sacraments in their entirety in infancy or by enrolling infants in a catechumenate and celebrating the rites later in adolescence, a position that causes some psychological trauma to parents, among others (Bausch, 108, 122).

The restoration of the unity of the rite of Christian initiation does not seem to be forthcoming at the present time, and therefore it is necessary to make provisions for pastoral practice. Following the general pattern set by the Pontifical Commission for the Revision of the Code of Canon Law of not resolving by legislation matters that are subject to debate, and noting that the National Conference of Catholic Bishops has made no attempts to restrict the variety of practices that exists in the United States, it would seem advisable that these guidelines not impose an authoritative settlement on the age for confirmation. Thus, the following guidelines seem appropriate until the National Conference concludes its own study and suggests an age for confirmation in this country:

- Flexibility in pastoral practice ought not be seen as negating the unity of the three sacraments of Christian initiation.
- Confirmation need not be locked into one age or grade level, except that the minimum age, that is, the age of discretion, determined by the Code of Canon Law and the Rite cannot be dispensed from.
- While theological, liturgical and catechetical study must continue, there need be no change in the present practice. In the Archdiocese of Saint Paul and Minneapolis, the present focus of this sacrament is with young people beginning at the age of discretion.
- Catechesis should be carefully adapted to the age group(s) of the recipients of the sacraments.
- Individual parishes should establish carefully prepared and clear policies on the question. The primary concern of such policies should be the careful presentation of confirmation as a sacrament of initiation.

THE SPONSORS.   The requirements regarding sponsors for confirmation are the same as for baptism (Canon 893):

- that they be named by the child's parents or guardians;
- that they be at least 16 years of age;
- that they be Catholic, themselves confirmed, already have received first communion, and lead a life in harmony with the duty that they are undertaking;
- that they not be one of the child's parents;
- that they not be bound by any inflictive or declaratory sentence to any canonical penalty (Canon 874, n. 1).

Ideally, the sponsors should be the same for both sacraments of initiation (Canon 893), thus expressing the unity of these two aspects of Christian initiation.

THE MINISTER OF CONFIRMATION. The bishop is the ordinary minister of confirmation (Canon 882). He may also grant to one or many presbyters the faculty to confirm. Both the bishop and the delegated presbyters can associate other presbyters with themselves, in individual cases, in the administration of the sacrament, should the need arise (Canon 884, n. 2).

In recent decades, we have seen a shift from the church's practice of reserving confirmation exclusively to the bishop. Priests have been given the faculty to confirm, in certain circumstances. In addition to the provisions of Canon 884, n. 2, the law itself (Canon 883, n. 2) empowers a priest to confirm adults when he baptizes them and adults and children of teachable age who are being received into full community with the Catholic church. This shift of discipline reflects the church's growing perception that baptism, confirmation and first communion are initiation rites and should be celebrated together and in sequence for adults and children.

THE COMMUNITY. Because confirmation is a sacrament of initiation, with initiation always understood as initiation into the Christian community, the celebration of the sacrament ought to take place in the midst of the community and with the community as involved as possible.

C. FORMAL CATECHESIS FOR CONFIRMATION

Because the practice regarding the age for confirmation varies, it is impossible to prescribe a single catechesis for the sacrament. After individual parishes have established guidelines for the age for the celebration of the sacrament of confirmation, they will then be able to develop appropriate programs of formation.

Special consideration must be given to those who are handicapped. The mere fact that an individual is handicapped by mental retardation does not preclude the possibility of receiving this sacrament. Mary Therese Harrington offers some practical insights in this regard:

> Because a person is mentally retarded, it does not mean that she or he does not have a form of reasoning. This may be global, not precise; not abstract; symbolic, not analytic. . . . What is important is that the person knows by participating in the action and probably not apart from it to any significant degree. The knowledge one has may be more participatory than theoretical.

Often the persons who are disabled cannot of themselves sort out what is *supposed* to happen. They can enter wholeheartedly into what *is* happening. They cannot generate much religious meaning related to the sacrament and apart from the experience ("Reflections on Participation in Sacramental Life," *Into the Christian Community* [NCEA, 1982], 34–35).

Though it is impossible to prescribe a single catechesis for the sacrament, some models of catechetical programs may be of help:

MODEL A:

Infant baptism, with confirmation and first communion celebrated around age seven. Here, the ordering of the sacraments follows the sequence set forth in the Code of Canon Law and the rites of the church. Confirmation thus completes baptism, and first communion completes Christian initiation.

The pastoral implementation of this model would call for a combined catechesis for confirmation and first communion. By offering this combined catechesis, the formation of children for the sacraments of Christian initiation would be attuned to the spirit of the Rite of Christian Initiation of Adults (RCIA), which describes a single, integrated catechesis for the three sacraments of Christian initiation. Preparation for the celebration of the sacraments provides a lived experience for their unity.

Catechesis for infant baptism would be directed to the parents and sponsors of the children to be baptized. Parents ought to be closely involved in the formation of their children for the celebration of the other two sacraments of initiation and in planning for their actual celebration. In those cases in which confirmation is celebrated around the age of discretion, there must be a recognition of the need for added rituals which express meaningful moments in the later lives of individuals—rites of passage. This need arises from the religious needs of adolescents and young adults. Such rituals could readily focus on the Sunday eucharist as the rite of Christian commitment for those who have completed Christian initiation. (The Appendix of the *Guidelines* for Saint Paul and Minneapolis includes models for such rites.)

MODEL B:
Infant baptism, with first communion celebrated around age seven and confirmation celebrated later, possibly even during high school years. Here, the ordering of the sacraments follows the sequence which reflects the current pastoral practice.

It would be necessary for the catechesis surrounding the sacrament of confirmation to emphasize that confirmation seals or completes the baptismal commitment. Preparation for confirmation is to be seen as a process of deeper Christian formation. The emphasis here would be on the adolescent stage of searching faith and on becoming a more active participant in the life and ministry of the parish community. In this model, catechesis would include more service to the community as well as a retreat experience.

In those cases in which confirmation is celebrated at a later age, especially when service to the community is seen as an important element in catechesis, confirmation as a gift must be stressed regularly, lest the sacrament of confirmation be seen as a reward either for service or for maturing. Any ministry to the community must be seen as formation for a life of service or ministry, not as a prerequisite for reception of the sacrament.

The following elements are common to the proposed models:
- Catechesis for confirmation, like the catechesis for baptism, takes place in the midst of the parish community (NCD, 117, 119);
- Parents and sponsors are intimately involved (Ibid.);
- Confirmation is seen as a sacrament of initiation, sealing the bond which begins in baptism (Ibid., 119);
- Baptism and confirmation lead to ongoing catechesis (Ibid., 117);
- The focus of this catechesis is on God's unending love (Ibid.);
- Immediate preparation involves a careful explanation of the rite and symbols related to the sacrament, so that its celebration can be a wholehearted experience (Ibid.).

INGREDIENTS OF CATECHESIS FOR CONFIRMATION

The Rite:	*Prayer:*	*Christian Acts:*	*Symbols:*
The ritual	Prayer	Prayer	Sign of the
Laying on of	The Lord's	Fasting	Cross on the
hands	Prayer	Service	forehead
Anointing	The creed	Welcoming	Anointing with
Sign of the	Litany	Study of	oil
cross		scripture	Water
Baptismal vows		Contact with	Oil
		the community	Candle
		of believers	
		Discipline	

D. CELEBRATION OF THE SACRAMENT OF CONFIRMATION

Ordinarily, confirmation is celebrated within the eucharistic liturgy to express more clearly the fundamental connection of this sacrament with the entirety of Christian initiation, which reaches its culmination in communion in the body and blood of Christ. The newly confirmed should then participate in the eucharist by which their Christian initiation is completed.

When confirmation is celebrated outside the eucharistic liturgy, emphasis should be given to the celebration of the word of God which begins the rite. It is from hearing the word of God that the many-faceted power of the Holy Spirit flows upon the church and upon each of the baptized and confirmed, and by this word God's will is manifested to believers. Whether the celebration takes place within or outside the eucharistic liturgy, the praying of the Lord's Prayer by the newly confirmed with the rest of the community is also of great importance, because it is the Spirit who prays within us, and in the Spirit the Christian is able to say "Abba, Father" (RC, 13).

The sacrament is conferred through the laying on of hands and the anointing with chrism. The whole rite has a twofold meaning: The laying on of hands is the biblical gesture by which the gift of the Holy Spirit is invoked; the anointing with chrism and the accompanying words express clearly the effects of the giving of the Holy Spirit. Signed with the perfumed oil, baptized Christians receive the indelible character, the seal of the Lord, together with the gifts of the Holy Spirit, which conform them more closely to Christ and give them the grace of spreading the Lord's presence among others (RC, 9). Because the proper symbols of confirmation are the laying on of hands and the anointing with chrism, "stoles" are not appropriate symbols for those being confirmed. The priesthood of all the faithful, conferred in baptism and complemented in confirmation, is different from, and not to be confused with, ministerial priesthood conferred in holy orders.

E. ONGOING CATECHESIS

The newly confirmed Christians, who now possess in a more complete way the life they received in baptism, need the support of their parents, sponsors and of the whole Christian community as they live out their life in the Spirit and their own ongoing conversion. The example of Christian living which they are able to see in these other Christians is an essential part of the ongoing catechesis that follows confirmation. It is primarily this experience of Christian living that will help them to serve as supportive witnesses to others, particularly those who are still in the process of Christian initiation.

Because conversion is a lifelong process, parish communities have the responsibility to provide their members with opportunities for continued biblical, spiritual and doctrinal formation, and for service to the community. When confirmation is celebrated with adolescents, it is important to recall that formation does not end with confirmation. The formation for confirmation is but part of an ongoing process of Christian formation.

Receiving Baptized Children of Catechetical Age into the Catholic Church

Often when adults are received into full communion with the Catholic church, they bring with them their children of catechetical age. In some cases, the children are unbaptized, and therefore it is necessary and appropriate for them to enter a catechumenate adapted to their abilities and needs; in other cases, they are baptized and need to be prepared for the other two sacraments of Christian initiation.

The "Christian Initiation of Children Who Have Reached Catechetical Age" (RCIA, 252–330) is intended for children, unbaptized as infants, who have now reached the age of reason, are able to be taught and have been brought by their parents for Christian initiation or have come of their own accord with parental permission (RCIA, 252). As in the case of adults, their formation takes place over an extended period of time (a number of years may be required in individual cases), and the various stages and periods of their initiation are enriched by liturgical rites. The RCIA is specific in noting that the adult Rite of Presentations (147–49, 157–63 and 178–84) may be used but should be adapted to children and that instructions and prayers ought to be adapted to their understanding (258).

The RCIA likewise sees the Easter Vigil as the appropriate time for the celebration of the sacrament of initiation for children (256) but is realistic in adapting that provision to the needs of the children involved.

It notes, for example, that, where necessary, the rite should be celebrated before a small but active gathering of the community, so that the children will not be upset by a large assembly (257).

The catechesis for these children is that described earlier in the chapter on the Christian initiation of children of catechetical age. It is important that such catechesis be adapted to the abilities and needs of the individual child. Their parents are to be as deeply involved in their formation as is possible.

These same principles apply in those cases in which children of catechetical age who have been baptized as infants, but have received no ongoing catechesis, are being prepared for the completion of their Christian initiation through the celebration of the sacraments of confirmation and first communion. Their catechesis must be carefully adapted to their existing faith development, needs and abilities. Their formation should move gradually, so that they may imbibe the richness of the life they will fully embrace in the celebration of these two sacraments.

CHAPTER 4

The Initiation
of Children:
The Path
One Parish Took

RICHARD P. MOUDRY

O N A SUNDAY MORNING in the Easter season this year, the bishop visited our parish and presided at our principal eucharistic assembly. All children who were ready for first communion received the sacrament of confirmation and then first communion from the bishop at that Mass.

This event represented a decision we made about how we might complete the initiation of Catholic children. After several years of studying the Rite of Christian Initiation of Adults and after much experience with our parish catechumenate, our staff concluded that our former practice of children's initiation (namely, baptism, first communion in the second grade and confirmation in the seventh grade) was for us no longer a satisfactory pastoral practice. So, in the fall of 1982, we invited the parents of children coming to first communion to allow the bishop to confirm their children in connection with first communion. After hearing and discussing the rationale for this change, a majority of parents chose to combine confirmation and first communion at the early age. That was the start.

Now, in our fifth year of parish catechesis on this practice, this pattern of initiation has become parish "policy." Now, it is rare for a parent to express serious objections or resist the practice.

Clearly, however, such practice does raise questions: What is the rationale for initiating Catholic children this way? How do we explain this change to parents? What convinced our parish staff to opt for earlier, instead of later, confirmation? Let me answer by addressing three issues that went into our decision. First, what insights does the history of Christian initiation provide about children's initiation? Second, how should we frame the question of confirmation practice today? Third, is our parish decision—early confirmation with first communion—the right one for us?

Our Parish Looks At History

We discovered that what we call "confirmation" today had a checkered history. After many centuries as a part of an integrated and unified celebration of Christian initiation, the bishop's "confirmation" rite gradually developed an identity of its own. Once separated from baptism and first communion, the rite of confirmation was practiced in different ways. Its initiatory focus was blurred. In fact, there have been times in the history of the church when confirmation as a sacrament disappeared completely from the lives of Catholics. Despite the checkered history, there is, I believe, a two-featured core to the confirmation tradition: 1) early confirmation; 2) confirmation before first communion.

Over the centuries the church has retained a deep religious instinct to offer initiation rites earlier in the life of a Christian, rather than later, and together, rather than separately. This is true not just in the Eastern church, which practices complete initiation in infancy to this day. It is also true in the Western church. In the West, baptism, confirmation, and first communion were celebrated together at Easter for adults and for children for centuries. As late as the 13th century such was the practice in the city of Rome. For centuries, infants were given communion of consecrated wine at baptism, and toddlers were allowed to share fragments at the eucharistic table when the adults went to communion. (In 1910, when Pope Pius X urged earlier first communion for children, he appealed to this practice of infant and children communion.)

Underlying this deep religious instinct is the conviction that three rites—water bath, anointing with imposition of the hands and admission to the table—are intimately connected to one another in what they mean and therefore in how they should be celebrated. Radically put, these three rites are one reality, not three realities. The newly baptized is anointed as the confirming of the baptism and as authorization to join the eucharistic assembly. Together, these three rites constitute the celebration of Christian initiation. The confirmation rite does not, on its own, have meanings and purposes different from or in addition to the meaning and purpose of baptism. Even when it happened that baptism was not immediately followed by confirmation, the popular religious instinct was to take the newly baptized child to the cathedral as soon as possible—within weeks or days or even the same Sunday afternoon if the bishop was near enough—for his anointing and imposition of hands. This instinct has never wholly disappeared in Latin cultures.

By the late Middle Ages, when confirmation and first communion were commonly celebrated apart from baptism, a two-step practice of initiation emerged for children of Catholic parents: 1) baptism at birth for newborn infants; 2) confirmation and first communion at about the age of reason. Despite many deviations from this pattern, the practice of two-step initiation—infant baptism completed with confirmation and first communion at about the age of seven—has remained the core of Catholic practice from the late Middle Ages until the present day.

In the countries of the world most influenced by the Protestant Reformation, Catholic practice tended to imitate that of the reformers by delaying the second step of initiation and by making confirmation-communion a catechetical, rather than an initiatory, event. Protestant "confirmation" stripped itself of any vestige of the Catholic understanding of confirmation as an initiation rite linked with baptism. Rather, "confirmation" was seen as the conclusion of childhood religious instruction and as a renewal of baptism. For that reason, "confirmation" also served as a rite of affirmation, which could be celebrated at various times in the life of a Christian. Protestants do not consider confirmation as a sacrament of the church, and today in many places the name "confirmation" has been dropped in favor of "affirmation."

From a historical perspective, we are probably the first generation of Catholics who would be surprised at the thought of celebrating confirmation before first communion. The reason we are so unique is that the practice of receiving first communion without previously being confirmed did not become an accepted practice in the church until the first part of the present century.

In 1910 Pius X urged that children be admitted to communion at the age of reason. The Pope's urging, however, did not constitute an authorization to invert the traditional sequence of the initiation sacraments. In fact, to prevent any such misunderstanding, in 1932 the Sacred Congregation of the Sacraments authoritatively interpreted Pius X's instruction by reaffirming that "children should not approach the sacred table for the first time until after the reception of the sacrament of confirmation." The congregation did allow, however, that in the special case of a child who did not have an opportunity to receive confirmation prior to communion, that child should be allowed to receive communion at the earlier age anyway. By the middle of the present century, this "special case" or exception or anomaly had become the common practice: first communion before confirmation. Even though such practice is historically recent, it has been accepted as the pastoral norm. As a result, ironically, confirmation before first communion—the normative sequence in the initiation tradition—registered on us as a deviation.

The Question of Confirmation Today

The decision about how to initiate our Catholic children was greatly influenced by how we shaped the question about current practice. Today, most Catholic dioceses and parishes practice later confirmation, and most curricula and sacramental preparation materials are directed to that practice. By "later" I mean at junior or senior high school age. Given the overwhelming historical evidence that points to earlier confirmation, we had to look closely at the rationale behind such practice.

The rationale for later confirmation is twofold. First, confirmation is often linked with religious education, that is with an ongoing catechesis during childhood to youth to a final ministry of preparation of candidates for the celebration of the sacrament of confirmation itself. The American Lutheran Church's 1970 definition of confirmation embodies this aspect of the rationale: "Confirmation is a pastoral and educational ministry of the church which helps the baptized child through word and sacrament to identify more deeply with the Christian community and participate more fully in its mission."

The second part of the rationale for later confirmation sees it as a commitment rite in which a person who was baptized in infancy now personally chooses to be a member of the church, professes a now internalized creed and commits herself or himself to adult responsibilities whose implications can be more fully grasped.

Since Vatican II, but based on this pre–Vatican II rationale, the age for confirmation has edged later and later as it gained greater meaningfulness as an independent commitment rite. At the same time that the age of confirmation was edging later and new confirmation ministry materials were being published, the *reform* of the sacraments called for by Vatican II was being promulgated. By the mid-1970s, these reforms were beginning to be explored and discussed for their pastoral implications, both catechetical and liturgical. Some of the insights of Vatican II we considered are as follows:

1. Baptism, confirmation and first communion are now to be understood as initiation rites, all three constituting Christian initiation, whether they are celebrated with adults or with children.
2. Confirmation, in particular, needs to be rethought and reshaped as an initiation rite and more closely linked to baptism for its meaning and practice. (The characterization of

confirmation as a commitment rite or as a rite of passage or related to a particular stage of human/faith development is without support in documents of Vatican II.)

3. The initiation sacraments are to be understood and celebrated in the traditional order—baptism, confirmation and first communion. This sequence and unity is explained as the liturgical expression of the church's understanding of what God did in Christ's act of redemption. There are no grounds in the reform for deviating from this principle when completing the initiation of children baptized in infancy.

4. There is no difference between the personal readiness required of a candidate for confirmation and that of a first communicant. In fact, readiness for confirmation is spoken of as the criterion of readiness for first communion. The idea that confirmation presupposes a need for greater maturity in the candidate than do baptism or first communion is without support in Vatican II. In celebrating initiation rites, readiness is always relative and takes different shapes depending on the age and condition of the candidates. There is no "objective" readiness, no capacity or level of maturity required by the meaning of the sacraments.

5. For Catholic children, the Latin tradition of a two-step initiation process is preserved: The initiation of children baptized in infancy (step one) should be completed by celebrating confirmation and first communion at about age seven (step two).

The question of confirmation for our Catholic children may be framed as follows: The recent practice of celebrating confirmation after and apart from first communion and the current movement towards later, high-school age confirmation are developments that are based on pre–*Vatican II* understandings of these sacraments. How, then, do we respond to Vatican II's extensive reform of Christian initiation, a reform that calls for a different practice—different from the common practice described earlier—and a practice that is based on a different theological rationale?

One response would be to begin to take steps to revise our understanding and practice of confirmation and first communion for Catholic children, so that gradually we also may begin to implement the reforms envisioned in Vatican II. This would be a task for pastoral leaders and religious educators, and it would have implications for publishers. Such a response might well involve the search for more appropriate rites: a rite of passage from childhood to adult membership in the church or a rite to mark an adolescent's movement to a new stage of faith development, the stage of questioning and searching.

Initiating Our Catholic Children

When it comes to the practical matter of deciding how to initiate the Catholic children of our parishes, the best options are not available. The Vatican II reform was comprehensive and radical when it dealt with the initiation of the unbaptized (adults or children of catechetical age) and when completing the initiation of baptized Protestants or fallen-away baptized Catholics. In many instances, for example, the reform permits the initiating priest to confirm in order to retain the linkage between baptism and confirmation and to ensure the initiation sacraments' traditional sequence—confirmation before first communion. But when it comes to the children of Catholic families, Vatican II was less explicit. True, the two-step practice of children's initiation dating from the Middle Ages (infant baptism to be followed later by confirmation and first communion at about the age of reason) was reaffirmed, but it leaves the initiation of our Catholic children impoverished, not yet expressive of the liturgical-theological values incorporated into the rest of the Church's reformed initiatory practice. For our Catholic children, the sequence has been restored, but the *unity* of the threefold initiatory event has not yet been recovered. Also, confirmation remains linked with first communion at the age of reason, still curiously separated from baptism. As a result, children born into practicing Catholic families today cannot be initiated as fully (unity *and* sequence) as can unbaptized children of catechetical age. Irony indeed.

Ideally, following the values of Vatican II, a Catholic child would be presented for initiation when the parents and the community were ready to initiate. At that time, whether the child be a newborn, a seven-year-old or a teenager, the initiation would be celebrated in its completeness: water bath, anointing with imposition of hands and first communion as the culmination of the event. Unfortunately, the Vatican II reform did not provide for this.

What about the policy change by which the Catholic children of our parish received confirmation and first communion at the bishop's Mass? I find our practice to have some advantages:

1. It is feasible under present church law.
2. It does not promote confirmation to the diminishment of baptism.
3. It highlights the initiatory meaning of confirmation and first communion.
4. Full eucharistic communion, not confirmation, is experienced as the culmination of initiation.
5. The catechesis about the meaning of the initiation of children harmonizes with the understanding of Christian initiation that is expressed in the catechumenate; thus one theology of initiation—not two—is operative in the parish.
6. The tasks of religious education, ministry to youth and the celebration of life passages are clearly separate from, following upon, and demanded by the completion of the initiation of our Catholic children.

To some, our parish policy of completing the initiation of Catholic children at the earlier age seems innovative and daring. Actually, it does no more than implement the directive of Vatican II—a modest step forward, a compromise and an intermediate (we hope) practice until the initiation of our Catholic children is more fully reformed.

CHAPTER 5

Now Confirmation Needs Its Own *Quam Singulari*

Linda Gaupin

I N THE FACE of the defensive catechetical preoccupations of the Counter-Reformation and the rigorist abuses of Jansenism, Pope Pius X promulgated the decree *Quam Singulari* in 1910 and effectively moved first communion from the teens to age seven. Maybe now is the time for a similar decree for the sacrament of confirmation.

It is certainly no secret that a great deal of controversy surrounds our current practices of confirmation. The good news is that we now have ample historical data available to enable us to examine the issues more thoroughly and thereby arrive at some informed decisions about our future practices of that sacrament.

One issue that needs to be addressed is sacramental order. The purpose of this article is to examine the question of sacramental order in light of history as it pertains to the relation of confirmation to eucharist.

Sacramental order does make a difference. It reflects and determines theological understanding and catechetical practice. Because of

this, it is critical that we carefully examine the theological and catechetical implications of confirmation received before or after first
communion.

History and Sacramental Order

In the first centuries of the church, the integral unity and sequence of
the initiatory sacraments were preserved. Eucharist was seen as the
sacrament of completion of the order of initiation.

The position of eucharist in the sacramental order marked it as the
sacrament of the "first fullness" of the Christian life. As such, it set the
path for all future Christian living.[1]

Not only did eucharist complete the initiatory process, but it was
also considered necessary for the salvation of the one being initiated.
Cyprian of Carthage chastised parents who allowed their children to
die without eucharist, and he warned them that they will be held
responsible on the day of judgment.[2]

All who were initiated in the early church, adults or infants,
completed their initiation with eucharist. This initiatory sequence was
upheld in the church even when candidates for initiation were exclusively children. In other words, baptism and eucharist were inseparable,
and baptism without eucharist was not initiation into the church.

Through the centuries, this foundational unity and order of
baptism, confirmation (which originally had no identity apart from
baptism) and eucharist was altered in two very different ways: 1) the
sacraments of initiation were often separated; 2) in Western medieval
and 20th-century Roman practice, their order was changed.

During the course of the Middle Ages, confirmation gradually
became separated from baptism and eucharist. For a careful discussion
of this separation, see J. D. C. Fisher, *Christian Initiation: Baptism in the
Medieval West.*[3] It is important for us to note two things: First, the
separation of baptism, confirmation and eucharist was not considered
the norm of the initiation practice of this period. Even as late as the 13th
century, when infant confirmation had become relatively uncommon,
there was general agreement that infant confirmation was still the goal.

This is shown in various local episcopal statements: "Though we understand that infant confirmation and eucharist is desirable, nevertheless, in our difficult times. . . ." Throughout late medieval times, clergy frequently warned the faithful that their children should be confirmed and that the parents should not wait long to do this.

Second, one of the reasons for the sporadic delay of confirmation during these centuries was a growing confusion among many of the faithful and some clergy about its purpose. They failed to see the necessity of having children confirmed because in most cases they had already been baptized and received the sacrament of completion and fulfillment, first communion.

A further separation of the sacraments of initiation took place around 1200 when eucharist was removed from the baptismal moment. This was part of a larger pattern. The faithful stopped receiving from the cup. Scrupulosity grew about the hard time infants had in swallowing the host.[4] In 1215, the Fourth Lateran Council decreed that communion was not obligatory until the "age of discretion."

The intent of the council was not so much to determine the age for first communion as it was to insure that the baptized faithful fulfill their obligation to receive communion by a certain age. In the process, first communion became linked with the phrase "age of discretion." The precise meaning of the phrase was not determined by the council and this ambiguity resulted in a wide variety of interpretations.

The separation of the sacraments of initiation did not result in a permanent change in the sacramental order, as is clear from the actions of the Council of Trent. It did, however, result in a long-lasting breakdown of the earlier unity of the initiatory sacraments. The three initiatory sacraments were now isolated from each other and left to flounder without an order that could provide a sense of continuity and meaning. This breakdown threatened the *initiatory* identity of the sacraments of confirmation and eucharist, setting them afloat, so to speak, without appropriate catechetical or pastoral roots. This opened them to the winds of popular piety and passing practice.

It was not until the 17th century that an order was reestablished for the reception of baptism, confirmation and eucharist. Following in the wake of the Protestant Reformation and the catechetical reformation set forth by the Council of Trent, the Roman church took a major step. It attempted to retrieve the initiatory character of the sacraments of baptism, confirmation and eucharist by uniting them within a tightly knit catechetical structure that once again restored them to their original order.

This catechetical reform took on three specific characteristics: 1) The school determined the shape of catechesis; 2) new manuals or catechisms became the major instrument; 3) catechized children became the principal product.[5] Because instruction of youth was seen as the strongest counter to the tensions created by the Protestant Reformation, the goal was to cultivate a living faith in early childhood through protracted catechesis. The practice was to stretch out the process of initiating children into Christianity.

This post-Reformation catechetical reform was structured in four major steps:[6] The first step began with the baptism of the infant. This was followed by catechesis in the home until the age of discretion.

The second step began with the child's entry into school, generally around the age of seven. During the school years, children were catechized for the reception of the sacraments of confirmation and penance. Catechesis for penance, however, was gradual and lasted for about four or five years.

The third step was devoted to the preparation of the child for first communion around the age of 12 to 14. With this post-Reformation reorganization of the catechetical structure, first communion once again was positioned as the sacrament of completion. Because it was seen as the fulfillment of Christian initiation for the child, the sacrament was celebrated in aspecial ceremony known as "First Solemn Communion" that identified the person as an adult in the Christian state. This solemn celebration focused on the initiatory character of the event with the renewal of baptismal promises around the font, a procession with lighted candles and the children dressed in white attire reminiscent of their baptismal commitment.

The fourth and final step of the process was directed towards ongoing catechesis into adulthood. This continuing education flowed from the catechetical preparation for first communion. Its object was to encourage lifelong study and the practice of appropriate duties.

The catechetical reform of the 17th century shows how the church coped with the problem of separating the initiatory sacraments. Though it was not an ideal solution to the problem, the reform did attempt to provide proper order and a semblance of sacramental unity. For the most part this structure remained intact until the 20th century.

Quam Singulari and Sacramental Order

One unfortunate result of the 17th-century catechetical reform was a later age for the reception of first communion. This late age, occasioned by post-Reformation catechetical concerns, was strongly "reinforced" by the rigorous demands for preparation and purity. Such demands flowed in large part from the influence of Jansenism, a popular theology with extreme emphasis on human sinfulness and unworthiness; Jansenism takes its name from the Dutch teacher Cornelius Jansen who died in 1638. It was this abuse associated with Jansenism that prompted Pope Pius X to the drastic action of *Quam Singulari* in 1910. In effect, the decree lowered the age for first communion to about seven and freed a child from lengthy, rigorist preparation.

The decree is important to our present situation for two reasons: First, it provides us with some insight into the catechetical and pastoral abuses associated with the initiatory sacrament of first communion. Citing our historical tradition, whereby communion was administered to infants, Pius X deplored the current practices that prevented young children from receiving it. He also condemned the further abuse whereby one age of discretion was assigned to the reception of penance and another to the eucharist. He stated: "To postpone communion, therefore, until later and to insist on a more mature age for its reception must be absolutely discouraged."[7]

The decree also condemned other abuses associated with the reception of the sacrament. These included the rigorist preparations required for first communion, making holy communion a reward for fulfilling excessive catechetical and spiritual practices. The decree explained that in ancient times communion was given to nursing infants; no extraordinary preparations were demanded of children.

Consequently, the decree mandated that a "perfect knowledge of things of the faith" is not required for first communion. An elementary knowledge suffices. Similarly the decree declared that a "full" use of reason was not required either, stipulating that only "some" use of reason was sufficient.

Second, *Quam Singulari* is important because of its implications for the sacramental *order* of confirmation and eucharist in the 20th century. In lowering the age of first communion to about seven, it left catechists with the pastoral dilemma of preparing children for the reception of confirmation, first penance and first communion at about the same time in the life of the child.

The decree created havoc in the United States as evidenced in many of the pastoral and catechetical journals of this period. In their attempts to implement the decree, pastors, catechists and publishers were at a loss in dealing with the problems the decree unleashed. In some places, confirmation was being received with first communion and in other instances not until the following year. The same was true of first penance.[8]

In their attempts to implement *Quam Singulari,* catechists soon realized that the previous catechetical model was no longer adequate. Instead of dealing with the questions of sacramental order, catechists saw themselves forced to face the catechism "improvements" needed to prepare a young child adequately for first communion. They saw that this had implications for all catechesis in the church. Soon, every effort focused on issues of catechetical structure, methodology, content and literature. This catechetical preoccupation continued for the next fifty years.[9] Consumed with the demands of this task, pastors and catechists have not yet asked the basic question of sacramental order.

Historical Insights

This history provides us with a context for some insights into the relation of confirmation to eucharist for children. First, there is a direct relation between sacramental order, theological understanding and catechetical practice. When first communion is received before confirmation, it loses its meaning as a sacrament of completion and fulfillment that marks the path for all future Christian living. Conversely, confirmation, received after first communion, is assumed to take on the function of marking this path.

Some say that confirmation is a sacrament seeking a theology, but this is true only if we persist in celebrating it out of order with baptism and eucharist. Confirmation has a rich theology and tradition—not as a sacrament of completion, which is the place of eucharist—but as a transitional sacrament between baptism and eucharist. Confirmation in this context seals what is begun in baptism and leads to the eucharist, the fullness and completion of the initiatory process.

When first communion comes *after* confirmation, the identity of the latter as the means of incorporation into the wider church, which was begun at baptism, is preserved. Reception of first communion *before* confirmation does violence to the meaning of both sacraments. Baptism is the way eucharist begins, and eucharist—not confirmation—is the way baptism reaches its fullness. Furthermore, eucharist—not confirmation—ritualizes most fully a person's mission in Christian life. In the concluding rites of the Mass, Christians are sent into life, to go out and live what they have just expressed as church.

Second, it is important not to confuse the *separation* of the sacraments of initiation with an *alteration* of their order (such as happened after the promulgation of *Quam Singulari*). The Council of Trent *restored* the order of baptism, confirmation and eucharist. And *Quam Singulari* dismantled that order—not so much by intention as by default. The reversal of the order of confirmation and eucharist by Pope Pius X was not given careful and systematic examination.

Third, *Quam Singulari* corrected the abuses associated with the practice of first communion. Perhaps we need a *Quam Singulari* for confirmation! Many of the practices formerly labeled abusive with the initiatory sacrament of eucharist still prevail today in our catechetical practices for confirmation.

We need to consider carefully the contradiction of a baptized child's right to first communion and first penance around the age of seven, *without* a corresponding right to confirmation at a similar age.

Quam Singulari condemned the distinction of one age of discretion required for penance and yet another age for first communion. We must contrast the wisdom of *Quam Singulari* with our recent trend to exact a later age for confirmation.

The catechetical situation of 1910 has many parallels in our current sacramental practices. Careful attention must be given to Pius X's refutation of the Jansenist abuse of excessive preparation for first communion. We often make confirmation a "reward" for attendance and preparation in a two- or three-year confirmation program. A perfect knowledge of the faith is not required for the two premier sacraments, baptism and eucharist. Yet we tend to require this for confirmation, using it as a catechetical ploy, a graduation ceremony that marks the end of a lengthy program of instruction.

Our catechetical practices for confirmation touch more than that sacrament alone. They have implications for our understanding of eucharist as well as for our entire initiatory policy in the church. The maintenance of a practice of only 80 years—one that has such profound implications—needs serious consideration.

Notes

1. For a detailed examination of the role of first eucharist in the initiation sequence see Linda Gaupin, *First Eucharist and the Shape of Catechesis Since "Quam Singulari,"* unpublished doctoral dissertation (The Catholic University of America, 1985), 11–78.

2. Cyprian of Carthage, "Treatise III: On the Lapsed," in *The Ante-Nicene Fathers,* Volume 5, edited by Alexander Roberts and James Donaldson, (New York: The Christian Literature Company, 1986), 437–47.

3. J. D. C. Fisher, *Christian Initiation: Baptism in the Medieval West* (London: SPCK, 1965).

4. Gaupin, *First Eucharist,* 54–61.

5. Mary Charles Bryce, OSB, "Evolution of Catechesis from the Catholic Reformation to the Present," *A Faithful Church,* edited by John Westerhoff and O. C. Edwards, Jr. (Hartford, Connecticut: Morehouse-Barlow Co., Inc., 1981), 216.

6. For a detailed history of the 17th-century catechetical reform, see Gaupin, *First Eucharist,* 96–122.

7. *Quam Singulari, AAS,* 2 (1910), 580.

8. William Costello, "Christian Doctrine for Public School Pupils," *The Ecclesiastical Review* 51 (December 1914): 665-67.

9. For more information on the impact of *Quam Singulari* on catechesis in the United States see Gaupin, *First Eucharist,* 204–37.

Bibliography

Austin, Gerard. *Anointing with the Spirit: The Rite of Confirmation* (New York: Pueblo Publishing Co., 1985).

_____. "What has Happened to Confirmation?" *Worship* 50 (1976), 420–26.

Balhoff, Michael J. "Age for Confirmation: Canonical Evidence," *Jurist* 45 (1985), 549–87.

Bernardin, Joseph Cardinal. *Access to the Sacraments of Initiation and Reconciliation for Developmentally Disabled Persons* (Chicago: Liturgy Training Publications, 1985).

Davis, Charles. *Sacraments of Initiation: Baptism and Confirmation* (New York: Sheed & Ward, 1964).

Gallen, John, ed. *Made, Not Born* (Notre Dame: University of Notre Dame Press, 1973).

Gusmer, Charles W. "The Revised Adult Initiation and Its Challenge to Religious Education," *Living Light* 13 (1976), 92–96.

Ivory, Thomas P. "The Restoration of the Catechumenate as a Norm for Catechesis," *Living Light* 13 (1976), 225–35.

Kavanagh, Aidan. *Confirmation: Origins and Reform* (New York: Pueblo Publishing Co., 1988).

————. "Confirmation: A Suggestion from Structure," *Worship* 58 (1984), 386–95.

————. *The Shape of Baptism: The Rite of Christian Initiation* (New York: Pueblo Publishing Co., 1978).

Keifer, Ralph. "Christian Initiation: The State of the Question," *Worship* 48 (1974), 392–404.

Kiesling, Christopher. *Confirmation and Full Life in the Spirit* (Cincinnati: St. Anthony Messenger Press, 1973).

Kung, Hans. "Confirmation as the Completion of Baptism," *Concilium* 9 (1974), 79–99.

McKenzie, Terri and Michael J. Savelesky. "Confirmation with First Communion? It Works!" *Catechumenate* 8 (May 1986), 16–23.

Moudry, Richard P. "The Initiation of Children: The Path One Parish Took," *Catechumenate* 9 (July 1987), 27–33.

Neunheuser, Burkhard. *Baptism and Confirmation,* translated by John Jay Hughes (New York: Herder and Herder, 1964).

Reedy, William J., ed. *Becoming a Catholic Christian: A Symposium on Christian Initiation* (New York: William H. Sadlier, Inc., 1978).

Roberto, John. "Confirmation in the American Catholic Church" (unpublished paper delivered in Washington at the National Conference of Directors of Religious Education, 1978).

Searle, Mark. *Christening: The Making of Christians* (Collegeville: The Liturgical Press, 1980).

————. "Issues in Christian Initiation: Uses and Abuses of the RCIA," *Living Light* 22 (1985), 199–214.

Yarnold, Edward. *The Awe-Inspiring Rites of Initiation* (London: St. Paul's Publications, 1971).